Extravagant Love

Craig Bullock

DEDICATION

This book is dedicated to my wife and best friend, Vicki Jo—
who embodies God's unconditional love..

CONTENTS

ACKNOWLEDGMENTS

This book is fruit of many lives. I am very grateful to my foster parents, Tom and Jean, for the love and generosity they continue to show me. I am the proud father of two wonderful sons, Nicholas and Michael—they have been and continue to be my spiritual teachers. I have an older sister, Giovanna, who is a great gift in my life. Daily, I am blessed by my Father-in-law Sam, and my Mother-in-law Lonnie. I have three wonderful step-children: Evan, Tori and Alana; their love helps to mend my heart. I am thankful to my longtime friend and theological partner in crime, Father John Colacino. This book would not have been written without the loving intervention of Father Bill and Father Bob. I am deeply indebted to the Notre Dame Sisters who administered Saints Peter and Paul's School—most especially Sister Minelpha and Sister Virginia. Without the help of my editors-Margaret, Julie and Renee-this book would never have come into form. I am very appreciative of the support I consistently receive from the Assisi Institute staff: Adam, Nancy, Purnima and Ursula. Last but not least, my heart goes out to the Assisi Institute Family—whose faith and love sustain me in many, many ways.

INTRODUCTION

As human beings, we are genetically programmed for maximum happiness. The source of our deepest, most authentic happiness is love. Real love, however, is not sentimental or romantic or dreamy. Rather, love is God and God is love. Thus, love is the most powerful force in all of creation—because it is the very energy of the Holy Spirit working to draw all of humanity into conscious union with God.

I have written this book, my personal story, for the sole purpose of bearing witness to the power of God's love. To the degree that we open ourselves to God's love, we give all of heaven permission to divinize our existence—to fashion our lives into living instruments of "truth" and "beauty" and "goodness."

As a young Catholic boy, I was introduced to God's love in many wonderful ways—most poignant among them was the "Breaking of the Bread," heroic stories of saints and the charge to live for others. These "windows" into God's love availed me to many moments of peace and joy and wonder. Yet, there remained a desire to stabilize the sense of Christ's loving presence, and to go deeper into the experience of

1

God-union.

As "providence" would have it, my desire for God-union took me in an unexpected direction--to the mystical traditions of India and to the teachings of a deceased Hindu monk, Paramahansa Yogananda. My journey to the East, however, did not divest me of my Christian roots. Paradoxically, if it were not for the grace-filled teachings of Yogananda, I would not be a Christian today.

Undoubtedly, some will accuse me of marginalizing Jesus and his message. If anything, I am attempting to open the eyes of readers to the expansive nature of his mission. Jesus is not a denomination but the embodiment of the "Cosmic Christ," the "mind of God," through whom all things and people were created. Thus, Jesus the Christ belongs to the whole world. His loving consciousness permeates every speck of creation—and is working to draw all people into the Divine Life. Am I stating that all spiritual paths reflect the same level of light? No! What I am saying, however, is that the consciousness of Christ is percolating in all places and times and people—seeking to reconcile humankind to God. In reading the Bhagavad Gita, for example, it is easy to recognize the very same wisdom that is at the heart and soul of the Judeo-Christian scriptures. God is indeed, One.

The fact of the matter is that we are living in an inter-spiritual age. Within a few doors of my own house lives a Hindu family, a Jewish family, an Evangelical Christian family, and around the corner a Muslim family. I am not suggesting we move towards a one world, singular religion. What I am saying however, is that we are all drawing life's water from the same spiritual well; and the "living water" that sustains me is the same "living water" sustaining my neighbors. The Holy Spirit is working, I believe, to create a sense of unity within the human family--so as to nurture a more loving, a more compassionate, and a more just world.

I still consider myself to be a son of the Catholic Church; and what I have discovered over the past twenty-years is that the Church possesses a rich and deep mystical tradition—just waiting to be broken open, so as to feed a world hungry for the direct experience of God. My prayer is that all who read this book will be blessed by God's unconditional and incomprehensible love. Peace!

1 God's Absolute Goodness

I have come that you may have life and life abundantly. - Jesus

God is love; His plan for creation can be rooted only in love. Every Saint who has penetrated to the core of reality testifies that there is a Divine, universal plan— that is beautiful and full of joy. -Yoganandaji

Wearing a tan dress shirt, maroon tie and dark pants, I was ready for my very first day of school. Of course, school began with Mass. Piously kneeling, hands folded in a gesture of prayer; I was doing my best to look as if I understood the Latin being spoken by the priest. Then it happened, from the depths of my being something began to stir within me. What was about to unfold was entirely out of my control. Taking a deep breath, I proceeded to vomit on my fellow students in the pew just in front of me. My first grade teacher, Sister Bernadette, quickly escorted me out of the Church.

"Are you feeling ill?"

4

"No Sister," I replied.

"You are just nervous. Don't worry. Someone is calling your parents. They will be here shortly."

Remembering stories from my older sister Giovanna concerning the strict nature of the nuns, I timidly asked Sister Bernadette, "Am I in trouble?"

Smiling, she placed her hand on my head and said, "No! You are not in trouble. God is good. You are good. We are all good. Get some rest; just don't stay away too long. We need your goodness." Her hand gently placed on my head produced a comforting, warm feeling within me. What felt even better were her positive words, affirming God's goodness.

If you are a Catholic of a certain age, you will undoubtedly remember the "Baltimore Catechism."[1] It was a manual of Christian belief and dogma, presented in a question and answer format-- which we were obliged to memorize or else suffer some ungodly fate. The very first question asked was, "Who made us?" Of course, the answer was, "God made us." This implied that our existence is not the result of a random roll of the cosmic dice. Rather, we have been loved into existence. Because God is love and we come from God, love is the very font and foundation of our existence.

On a practical level, we are hardwired for love—meaning that buried in deepest depths of the human spirit is the memory of loving union. As a psychotherapist, I am always amazed at the fact that so many people are unwilling to give up on love.

---

[1] The "Baltimore Catechism" was the de facto standard religious text for schools in the United States from 1885 to the late 1960s

Even after multiple divorces, men and women are willing to give marriage another try. Literally, we are fashioned for love.

At some time or another, we have all caught a glimpse of a larger and loving dimension, a higher world, or a heavenly realm—even if it is only out of the corner of our eyes. In these moments of breakthrough, we invariably feel whole, complete and loved. Intuitively, we know we are part and parcel of a "Reality" that is infinitely good and loving. Whether we can name it or not, we experience ourselves as being in a state of loving communion with God.

Consciously or unconsciously, we are haunted by these moments of breakthrough. Virtually all of human behavior is motivated by a hunger for loving happiness. Whether we can name it or not, it is God's truth, beauty, and goodness that we are hoping to rediscover. Even when we look for happiness in all the wrong places, we are actually looking for God. This is why nothing is more damaging to the human spirit than the loss of hope—hopelessness is the belief that we will never experience our soul's desire, loving union.

Seven years after Sister Bernadette escorted me out of Church; my abiding hope in God's goodness suffered a serious blow. Due to complications related to Leukemia, my beloved mother died. This left me in the care of a kind, but profoundly alcoholic father. My mother's strength was the organizing glue to our family life. Instinctively, I knew that the next few years were going to be hellish in nature. For the first time in my life, hopelessness engulfed my tender heart.

Surprisingly, I experienced a ray of hope during my mother's funeral Mass. Though I was sitting between my somber father and my weeping older sisters, I still felt very alone. There was no contact between us, emotionally or otherwise. The whole family was lost in a deep, dark grief. As the priest began his homily, I felt a sense of relief. There was something other than my pain to focus on. I did not understand most of what he had to say, except the following words, "Yes, this is an occasion for sorrow, but also for joy. For your mother is resting in the loving arms of God, and you have the hope of being reunited with her in heaven."

Immediately, I imagined my mother being hugged by God. I thought to myself, "No more hardships for her." My heart opened and I felt a sense of relief. Then the thought came to me, "If I'm really good, I'll get to go to heaven and see my mother again. I'm going to try hard to be good. I think I can do it." Feeling lighter myself, I expected my family would also be feeling uplifted by the priest's message. But when I looked at each of them, they were all still stuck in their grief. So I kept my hope to myself, where I knew it would be safe.

The next two years unfolded as I had feared they would. My father's alcoholism deepened, home life became increasingly chaotic, and the family splintered into many different and isolated directions. Much of my attention focused on sports and my friends. What sustained me more than anything else, however, was the comfort and support I received from my Catholic world. For example, I would periodically spend Saturday afternoons at the parish convent, doing chores for the nuns. My primary motivation for doing so was the peace I felt within the convent, and the loving appreciation they showed me upon the completion of my duties— often in the form of cookies and milk. Despite the structure and support my parish offered me, it was not enough to overcome the chaos of my home life. Essentially, I was raising myself.

At some point during the seventh grade, I entered puberty. Besides the obvious changes that accompany such a transition in a young man's life, my attitude began to shift. My easygoing nature gave way to negativity, moodiness, and a certain level of aggression. I was getting into more and more fights, and could be cruel to my friends. Increasingly, I was doing whatever I wanted. I was also becoming angrier and angrier at God— blaming "Him" for all of my misfortune. More and more, I distanced myself from anything having to do with church. My innocence was quickly evaporating, along with my sense of hope.

As I was about to enter the eighth grade, I decided to leave the confines of my Catholic world. I still had a passion for sports and desperately wanted to play football. To play football, however, you had to be in the ninth grade. So just a few weeks prior to the start of football season, I went to the local public high school to enroll for the upcoming school year--as a ninth grader. The woman in the office was so focused on painting her nails and chewing her gum that she never made eye contact with me. She just handed me the papers and told me to "fill them out." When I gave them back to her, she said "Thank you, young man," blew a bubble, and put the papers in a drawer. No one from the school called my former school to verify my status, and it was impossible to call my home because we had no phone. For all practical purposes, I was a freshman in high school.

I was able to get away with these kind of actions for the reason that my Father was either working or spending nights at his girlfriend's house. When we were together, he was most often drunk. I had no real supervision. Even when he did try to rein me in, I simply ignored his edicts and did whatever I wanted to do.

I was big and strong for my age and was able to make the junior varsity football team. After football season ended, I made the wrestling team— even going undefeated for the entire season. While my athletic career was booming, my academic life was non-existent. I never attended classes with any regularity. I would get up when I wanted, do what I wanted, and made it to school in time for practice. My teammates would jokingly refer to me as a "professional athlete," because I rarely attended classes.

After wrestling season ended, I stopped going to school altogether. I was increasingly unable to relate to my long term friends, who went to school every day and came from relatively stable families. I was feeling lost and alone. A fellow member of the wrestling team invited me to hang out with him and his friends. His neighborhood had a reputation for violence, drugs, and organized crime— an Italian barrio of sorts. I saw it as a chance to belong, to have an identity, to be a part of something bigger than myself. I consciously tried to fashion myself into a 'thug" or "tough guy."

I was quickly accepted into this new group of friends. Most of them had quit school and were older than myself. Our activities centered on drinking, fighting and carousing. The "kingpin" of the neighborhood was a fellow named Tony. Tony was in his mid-twenties, had already done time in jail, and was rumored to be connected to the Mafia. He was funny and very tough. No one ever challenged him. Tony took somewhat of a liking to me, which made me happy. I saw him as a kind of hero, someone I wanted to emulate. Occasionally, he would ask me to run errands for him. I was glad to please him.

On a warm summer day, we were hanging out, making fun of each other, and laughing. Then Tony showed up. He was not in his typical prankster mood. Quickly, we all became quiet. Tony asked in a serious tone, "Will you do something for me"

"Sure Tony," I answered.

"See that family moving in across the street?" he asked.

"Yea," I answered.

"I don't like them. They're not good for the neighborhood. I want you to go and start a fight with the kid in the driveway. He's about your size, but you can take him."

I responded, "But he didn't do anything to me."

He shot back, sternly, "Just do it."

Not wanting to displease him, I walked across the street, pushed the kid and we both started throwing punches. Fortunately, the fight was quickly broken up by neighbors. Later Tony told me, "We gave them a message" and that he was "proud" of me. I smiled on the outside, but on the inside I felt bad, real bad. I knew what I did was wrong, and that my mother would not be proud of me. I never returned to that neighborhood again. Ten years later, Tony was killed in one of the local Mafia wars.

The next four or five months were spent unproductively. I had series of part-time jobs, none of which I was able to keep. I avoided getting into legal trouble, but still felt lost and aimless. One Sunday morning, just a few days before my sixteenth birthday, I woke up and decided to attend Mass. Mind you, I had not been to church in two or three years. I was simply desperate. I was still not attending school; I was semi-homeless and feeling quite lost. I needed something "greater" than myself to do for me what I could not do for myself.

During Mass, I remembered the spiritual lessons learned in my Catholic school days, "God was good and all-powerful." So I placed my attention on a life-sized crucifix hanging next to the main alter, and prayed to Jesus: "If you are who they say you are, please help me, because I am lost."

Immediately after Mass, Father Bill, the priest who presided at my mother's funeral approached me. After exchanging pleasantries, he asked if I was interested in attending a retreat for teenagers. Feeling like I had nothing to cling to in my life except my toughness, and there is nothing tough about a retreat, I instinctively replied, "No thanks, Father."

To which he responded, "If you attend the retreat, whatever it is you are looking for, you will find it. I promise."

Then it hit me, *"Maybe this is an answer to the prayer I had just prayed in church."* Feeling a flash of hope, I answered, "Okay "Okay Father, I'll go."

Two weeks later, my enthusiasm for the retreat had waned. Things were going good with my girlfriend and I was offered a job at a local restaurant, washing dishes. I felt less desperate. The day before I was to attend the retreat, I called Father Bill to let him know I could not make it because of my new job. He was disappointed, while I was relieved. My tough guy image was intact, so I thought.

However, God was not to be denied. A few hours later Sister Virginia— the nun who taught my seventh grade class— called me. "Hi Craig, this is Sister Virginia."

"Why are you calling me at my girlfriend's house?" I asked.

"I called your boss at your new job, and he said you could start working when you return from the retreat. Isn't that good news?" "

Yes, sister," I said, in a less than enthusiastic tone.

Months after attending the retreat, I discovered that Sister Virginia not only prayed for me while I was on the retreat, she fasted from all food the entire three days of the retreat, just for me. God is good, and so are His helpers.

The retreat began in a rather challenging manner. Four of my friends also attended. Having brought a supply of marijuana with them, they were hardly engaged in the retreat. As for myself, the first day of the retreat I bounced back and forth between my friends and the formal activities.. Nothing my friends were doing actually appealed to me. It felt like empty stupidity. Yet, I was not sure I wanted to join the group of straight-laced, college bound suburbanites either. *"I have nothing in common with them," and I do not want to let go of my tough guy image."* I thought to myself.

However, things began to shift for me on the last night of the retreat. I decided to completely ditch my friends and give the program a try. The evening began with the staff members sharing their stories. There was one guy in particular who caught my interest. Though a bit older than me, he was from the city and had clearly experienced the darker side of life. And at the same time, he talked about knowing God "personally" and that God had worked "miracles" in his life. Something in me opened up. I thought to myself, *"If that cool guy can find God and still be cool, maybe I can find God and still be tough." And if God worked miracles in his life, maybe God can work miracles in my life."*

What followed was a beautiful candlelight penance service— in the context of a soft, warm and safe atmosphere. Inside of my heart, I was feeling hope, hope that my life could be different, hope that God was real and hope that good things could happen to me. I made the decision to go to confession.

Once in the makeshift confessional, I said to the priest, "I don't want to focus on my sins. I just really want to give myself to God, I really do. I just don't know how."

After chuckling, he told me to go to my room and get on my knees. "Pray to God to come into your life, to give you a new life, to give you strength to do what is right. Do this not only tonight, but each day when you wake up and when you go to bed at night."

I did just as the priest had told me to do. I went to my room, got on my knees, and prayed, "God, I need you. My life is a mess. I give my life to you." At first, a wave of peaceful silence settled over me. It felt good. I thought to myself, *"Wow, this prayer stuff really works."* Then, the peaceful silence gave way to a sense of presence, a big presence-- God's presence. I was enveloped in love. I felt whole and complete, and all was well in my world. Words came to me, not out loud, but intuitively--bubbling up from the depths of my own heart, I heard "If you give your life to me, it will never be the same."

The remainder of the night I felt part of something large and powerful and good. I experienced myself as actually being in light, in love, in God. For the first time in a long time I felt a sense of safety and security, that there was a plan, and that everything was going to be alright. Eventually, I fell asleep into the arms of a God who felt like the very essence of love.

Upon returning home from the retreat, I began every day on my knees, praying for help and strength. And I ended every night on my knees; thanking God for the grace He had given me that day. In between, my mind naturally turned towards God. You could even say that I was prayerfully obsessed with God— I had to be in order to get through my days, my doubts, and my temptations.

Not too long after being home, challenges came my way. The more I immersed myself in spirituality, the more my friends ridiculed me. One evening I walked into a social gathering and immediately they dropped to their knees and started bowing to me. At first it was kind of funny, but they kept on doing it. And when my friends finally stopped, they seriously tried to encourage me to return to my old life. The more time

I spent with them, the more fragile my new found faith became. After praying about the matter, I realized a choice had to be made. I needed to break off these friendships.

Naturally, I gravitated to our parish youth group. We would meet weekly— on a Saturday night for prayer, scripture study, Mass and pizza. I sincerely cherish the memories of these gatherings. The sense of God's presence was almost always palpable, and we were very loving and supportive of one another. When we were not meeting formally at church, we hung out together-- playing football, watching sporting events, and talking about girls. Most of the youth group members had taken part in a retreat similar to the one I attended— meaning we shared a common faith experience. Without the sense of community I felt with these new friends, I would not have made it through this difficult transition.

Almost daily, I attended Mass. In the "Breaking of the Bread," I experienced myself as being in the company of Jesus. It was this "Eucharistic grace" that helped to sustain me. In addition, I went to "confession" weekly. While in the confessional, I often felt what I experienced on the retreat— a sense of God's enveloping, protective presence. I started reading as much spiritual material as I could get my hands on; most of it being scripture and the lives of the saints.

I started attending a school for dropouts— actually discovering that I liked learning and that attending college was a real possibility. Yes, things were really looking up, until one painful day. I had been living with a friend and his family. Unexpectedly, the father of the household told me that I should go back to living with my father. What he did not realize, and I was too ashamed to admit, was that living with my father was not an option, at all. So I simply packed my belongings into a plastic bag and left--with no place to go.

Having about $150 in my pocket, I spent the first part of the night in a local all-night diner. I kept on ordering various dinners so that they would not kick me out. Finally, the emotional pain became more than I could endure. I wanted to feel better— anyway that I could.

Just a few blocks away there was a strip of road inhabited nightly by many prostitutes. I decided I would go and pay for sex. I just wanted to stop hurting. Upon arriving at my ill-reputed destination, there were no ladies to be found, not one. I waited and waited and waited, still no ladies arrived. Finally I gave up and spent the remainder of the night walking around the city, in a confused stupor.

As dawn approached, I headed for church— knowing that I could attend an early Mass, if for no other reason than to get warm. Immediately after, Father Bill approached me, "There is talk that you spent the night on the street."

Avoiding eye contact, I answered, "Yes Father."

"Well," he replied, "you don't look much worse for the experience. God's angels must have been protecting you from trouble. Bring your stuff over to the rectory and get some breakfast. Until we come up with a permanent plan, you can live there."

I have often reflected on Father Bill's statement, "God's angels must have been protecting you." Part and parcel of the Catholic ethos is a staunch belief in an unseen world, replete with saints, angels, powers and principalities--whose job it is to guard us in and through our hazardous earthly challenges.

Human life is meant to be lived in the context of mystery, grace, and a higher, celestial realm. Jesus taught us to pray, "Our Father in heaven, hallowed be your name. Your kingdom come, your will be done, on earth as it is in heaven."[2] Our physical world exists within a larger, spiritual dimension. Even modern physics admits to this possibility.[3] We cannot hope to change the world or ourselves via human will power or cleverness. No, there must be a breakthrough of grace and wisdom and power from a higher dimension— the kingdom of heaven--into our everyday lives.

I believe that my "guardian angel" was protecting me on that painful night many years ago. Can it be explained? Not really. Can it be proven? No. It is just known, intuitively. When Peter made his proclamation of faith, *"You are the Christ, the son of God."* Jesus responded, *"Blessed are you Simon Bar-Jona! For flesh and blood has not revealed this to you, but my Father who is in heaven."*[4] Spirituality is not merely another ideological structure, but the loving eruption of the miraculous into our everyday lives—a mystery that can only be experienced, but never wholly explained. This marriage of heaven and earth takes place within our own hearts, and elevates us above instinct, habit, and karma—initiating us into the "Divine Life."

Saint Paul tells us, "Eye has not seen, ear has not heard, nor has it even dawned on man what God has prepared for those who love Him."[5] This means that we can only live a truly human life to the extent that we avail ourselves to God's energy, grace and power. If we want to fulfill our potential to live creatively, generously, lovingly and fearlessly, we must do so in God, through God, and because of God.

The "Good News" is that the "Kingdom of God is at hand,"

---

[2] The Gospel of Matthew: chapter 6, verse 10.

[3] For example: "String Theory" is a mathematically consistent model of physics that is considered to be a complete theory of everything; and it theoretically posits at least ten different but related dimensions.

[4] The Gospel of Matthew" chapter 16, verses 16-17.

[5] 1 Corinthians, chapter 2 verse 9

meaning that God is always with us— inviting us into deeper and deeper levels of loving communion. This has nothing to do with perfecting the personality, at all. We are loved not because we are good, but because God is good. God simply waits for our "yes" to His ever-present, unconditional "Yes" towards us.

2 God's Wise, Loving and Purposeful Providence

Not even a sparrow falls to the ground without the Father's consent. – Jesus

He who perceives Me everywhere and beholds everything in Me never loses sight of Me, nor do I ever lose sight of him. - Bhagavad Gita

Life in the rectory unfolded rather naturally. The three priests already living there were kind and supportive—and tough when they needed to be. I continued in my studies, my faith life deepened and I was feeling quite at home in such a spiritual environment. My life was stabilizing and I was feeling good. Then early one June morning I got the news, Father Bill was being transferred to the other side of the country. In fact, all three of the priests were being reassigned. This meant, of course, I had to vacate the rectory.

To his credit, Father Bill tried hard to find alternative housing for me, but to no avail. With no other options in sight, I was made a ward of the local county. Just a few days before he was to leave town, Father Bill dropped me off at my new home--an institution for "wayward boys." It was a sad moment for both of us. Before getting out of his car, Father Bill asked, "Are you alright?"

I responded with a stoic one word answer, "Yes."

He then asked, "Do you have your bible?"

"Yes", I answered..

With a mix of tenderness and strength, Father Bill gave me my marching orders, "Remember to pray every day." I simply nodded in agreement. He continued, "Trust God, things are going to work out. I know it."

Though I did not feel it at that moment, I believed that he believed it. I answered, "Yes Father."

We hugged. I got out of the car and walked alone into my new home. During the first meal, a fight broke out between a resident and a staff member, amidst the cheers of the other guys. I realized they thrived on chaotic, combative situations. At that very moment, I thanked God for my large, muscular two-hundred pound body. It encouraged the guys to leave me alone—which was fine with me because I had no desire to interact with them. When I wasn't doing chores, I simply stayed in my room. I just did what was expected of me, avoided eye contact with others and minded my own business—so as to avoid any confrontations.

Alone in my room at night, I would undergo a certain degree of sadness. Invariably, I would pray and read my bible. On more than one occasion, I experienced a profound spiritual presence—no voices or visions, just a palpable presence. I believed and continue to believe that it was the grace of Jesus' presence that sustained me. It was as if his consciousness was permeating my awareness. It was strong, wise and loving. To know Christ is to love him. Words cannot express what I experienced, nor do they capture the gratitude I continue to feel for such unmerited consolations. Literally, I owe my life to the love Jesus showered on me during this challenging period of my life. In recalling these experiences, however, I must admit to a certain level of sorrow or regret. So much grace has been given to me, and subsequently I feel as though I have wasted much of it. All that I can do is go forward, seeking to do God's will.

Not long after moving to my new home, I visited a priest from a nearby town. Upon telling him of my new living situation, he immediately answered, "I had a conversation with a wonderful family earlier today, a good Catholic family. They told me they were interested in providing a loving home for a teenager in need. They live in the country, on a farm."

In record time I answered, "Thanks but no thanks. There is no way I am moving from the city to a farm, in the middle of nowhere."

The priest paused, and then spoke in a very authoritative tone, "This is God's will. I know it. I just know it."

I replied, "Yes Father. I will pray about it. I promise."

Eventually, arrangements were made for an overnight visit. Then another visit—at the end of which the mother of this large, Irish Catholic family asked, "When are you going to come live with us?"

Hand on my hips, "That's kind of a bold question."

"Not really, the moment I saw you I loved you as if you were my own biological child."

I was stunned by her proclamation of love, and also deeply moved. So as to hold back my tears and to not show any vulnerability, I simply said "Yes."

After some legal hurdles were overcome, I moved into my new family's home on July 3rd, my deceased mother's birthday. To be honest, I was positively awed by my new abode. It was clean, orderly and large-- surrounded by trees, open fields, gardens, a large pond and other natural scenes. There was even a family dog, a beautiful German Shepherd. In addition, I had become the oldest brother of six new loving younger children. Did it all feel like a dream? Yes, a gracious, loving dream hatched in the mind and heart of God.

Though there were many valuable lessons to emerge from my new life, none were more significant than a deepening appreciation for the living and dynamic reality of "God's will," otherwise known as "Divine providence." Saint Paul tells us that "We live, move and have our being in God."[6] This means that we exist in God—which is to say that our lives unfold within the nest of God's purposeful, intelligent, and all powerful love. In other words, we are not in charge of much, at all. Not only are we not in charge, God uses all events and circumstances so as to serve a definite purpose— our spiritual evolution, to be exact.

To quote the late Father Jean-Pierre De Caussade, "We must put all speculation aside, and with childlike willingness, Accept all that God presents to us. What God arranges for us to Experience at each moment is the best and holiest thing that could happen to us."[7]

---

[6] Romans: chapter 17, verse 28.

[7] "Abandonment to Divine Providence," written by Jean-Pierre de Caussade, The book written by a 17th century Jesuit priest is one of

Jumping ahead chronologically, I had a life-altering conversation with a wonderful priest who has served as a spiritual father of sorts.[8] I was somewhere in my early thirties when the conversation occurred. Out of nowhere he stated, "It was a good thing that you had the childhood you did."

Dumbfounded, I shot back, "How can you say such a thing. You know the deprivation I experienced as a child. I am spending thousands of dollars each year in psychotherapy, so that I can heal my childhood wounds and have a chance at real happiness. I'm shocked by what you're saying."

In a calm voice he answered, "Listen, I know you had a traumatic childhood. I get it. You are a very bright and gifted man. If you were not wounded you would probably just be a rich yuppie, making lots of money, and contributing nothing to the world. Because you're wounded, you've become a wounded healer, making a real difference in the world. Perhaps you were meant to have the childhood you had."

---

the best kept secrets in the Catholic Church. A must read for those who are serious about their spiritual life. One of five or six books I would want to have with me if I were on a desert island. It situates all of history within the field of God's loving providence, meaning that events and circumstance actually serve our highest, noblest evolution—regardless of whether or not we understand it to be so. It gently dethrones us from life's center and acknowledges the rightful place of God I the universe's evolutionary process.

[8] The priest who has served as a spiritual father is Richard Rohr, OFM. The debt of loving gratitude I feel for him is immeasurable. Unfortunately, there are a dearth of fathers and mothers in the Church today. Without the wisdom and guidance of a spiritual mentor, the pitfall on the spiritual path can prove to be dangerous and overwhelming.

Quite honestly, that conversation was the beginning of the end of my need for psychotherapy. If my childhood was part of a providential plan, then I was not a victim. Nothing happens to us, only for us. I literally stopped asking "Why, why, why?" Instead, I gradually cultivated the practice of saying "Yes God" or "Thy will be done" or "As you wish God." In short, the ultimate spiritual practice is the surrendering of our personal will to God's will, at all times and in all places.

Though I had enjoyed visiting the farm, living there was something else altogether. Farm life was good, but challenging. Hard work was a way of life. I was stretched to learn foreign skills, and I deeply missed my old friends. And, there were rules to follow. To top it off, I tore up my knee on the third day of football practice—requiring surgery. There were times during that first year when the urge to bolt was very strong. I often dared myself to pack my bags and head to the old, familiar neighborhood.

What kept me on the farm, however, was a persistent intuition that it was God's will that I remain. I did not want it to be God's will. I just knew that it was part of the plan. I also knew that God's will always serves our highest good—resulting in our ultimate happiness. Once we step outside of God's will, we only increase our suffering. So through prayer, bible study and spiritual direction, I found the strength, courage and grit to stay. In addition, I was falling in love with my new family. I knew leaving them would break their hearts, and I could not bring myself to do such a thing.

The notion of God's will, however, was not easy for me to initially accept. My impulse was to make things up as I went along, to create my own reality, and to define "truth" for myself. I remember being fascinated with a deistic notion of God—that though there might be a God, He was not literally involved in my day-to-day life. If that were true, then I was more or less free to craft my own path through life. But in my heart, I absolutely believed that God was intimately involved in the details of my life, and that it was in my best interest to stay faithful to God's will.

We must remember that in Jesus' , God did not merely send the world a benign Christmas greeting. Rather, God entered into the core of the human drama as a loving, organizing and transforming presence. *"The Word was made flesh and dwelt among us."*[9] This means that God abides not only in the great cathedrals of the world, but in the nook and crannies of our lives—not as a disinterested bystander, but as the momentum of Truth, Beauty, and Goodness. God has penetrated into the heart of the human drama so as to gather us, and all the aspects of our humanity, into the Divine Life. There is no other way to become truly, deeply human.

After being with my new family for a month or two, I met a cute, dark-haired Italian girl at my new parish church. By her flirtations and frequent notes, it was easy to surmise that she was interested in me, and I was certainly interested in her—if for no other reason than she was interested in me and very pretty. Being a sixteen year old male, it did not take much to capture my imagination and heart. Naturally, I began to pursue her in the hope that she would become my steady girlfriend.

Not long into my courting dance, my "new father" took me aside to discuss a "matter of importance." He began the conversation with the following request, "I am asking you to avoid getting into a dating relationship, for now."

Incredulous, I responded, "Why?"

---

[9] The Gospel of John, chapter 1, verse 14.

To which he calmly replied, "You are still connecting with the family, and it is important that you bond with us. If you bond with a girlfriend right now, you might not bond with us. We want to make sure you become one of us before you dive into a romantic relationship. Does that make sense?"

I nodded my head in agreement, but inwardly, I was not happy at all. I wondered, *"Who is he to tell me what to do. When did God die and leave him boss? Does he know who he is talking to?"*

I took my interior protestations to my spiritual director, a wise and savvy priest. After pleading my case to him, the priest responded with a series of questions: "Is he a good, prayerful man?" "Does what he said make sense?" "Do you think he has your best interests in mind?" And do you think God has placed him in your life as an authority over you?"

Believing that God was directing my life, I answered "Yes" to his questions, even the last one.

Fixing his eyes on mine, He stated emphatically, "Obey!" When I tried to protest, he persisted in chanting the same mantra, "Obey! Obey! Obey!" Finally, I shut my mouth and left our meeting in silence, fuming but determined to "Obey."

I can't say I was always perfectly obedient to my new father, but I did learn to trust his authority. And in trusting his authority, something surprising occurred. I experienced a consistent level of peace, happiness, and security. In opening myself to my father's legitimate authority, I came to realize that I was not on my own, holding up my life all by myself. I was part of something bigger and larger and grander than myself. I was literally living within a "gravitational field" of strength and wisdom and love—what Jesus referred to as the

"*The kingdom of heaven.*"[10] I was free to let go, to rely on a power greater than myself, to love, to play, to take risks, to laugh, to be happy, to be fearless. I was free to be what Jesus asks all of us to be, a mere child resting in the Father's love.[11]

A story from my Catholic school illustrates this process in a clear and humorous manner. On a warm October day, I emerged from the neighborhood shoe repair shop feeling invincible, on top of the world, like a big man; mind you, I was all of eleven years old. I had just gotten a pair of steel taps on my school dress shoes. Every step I took proudly and loudly announced my presence. I was officially one of the tough guys, a future leather-jacketed hood, to be sure. I was convinced my classmates would deem me the coolest kid in the class.

The next morning, I didn't just walk into my classroom; I strutted into my tiny kingdom, fully expecting to hear sounds of admiration, praise and envy from my fellow students. Instead, I heard sister Minelpha's voice, "Hey, mister big shot, come over here." Before I knew it, I was facing my entire class, with the good Sister standing next to me. "Mr. Bullock thinks he is a big shot. Well, if Mr. big shot wants to stay in this school, he will get those taps taken off his shoes, today. Is that clear Mr. Big shot?"

A chorus of laughter erupted from my classmates.

---

[10] Jesus gave the "kingdom of God" a central place in his teachings. Miracles accompanied his proclamation of God's kingdom, along with exorcisms. The kingdom of God represents the in breaking of God's love and energy into human history as a transforming and elevating and organizing power—empowering us to live the divine life here and now. In order to be open to grace of God's kingdom, one must align one's life to God's will.

[11] Mark 10:15

Next, Sister enlightened me with her sage advice, "Listen, you are a good boy. Just don't get carried away with yourself. God is bigger than you, bigger than me, bigger than all of us. It is His bigness that matters, not our imagined bigness. Be humble and acknowledge God in all things and you will have a good life.... Now take off those stupid shoes and sit down."

Aligning to God's will is not a matter of stoic willpower. Rather, it is the process of nurturing a consistent willingness to be in flow of God's wisdom and grace. Scientists tell us that nature abhors a vacuum. God, on the other hand, is drawn to humble emptiness. The intuitive knowing of God's will--and the power to carry it out--effortlessly arises in a heart that is open, simple and naturally empty. The very first beatitude of Jesus makes this very clear, "*Blessed are the poor in spirit, for the kingdom of heaven belongs to them.*"[12]

Without a degree of solitude, it is impossible to be consistently and deeply aligned to the flow of God's will. One of the challenges of living on the farm was the fact that I was socially isolated. All of my schoolmates and potential friends lived in town, while I lived in the country. At times, I was quite lonely.

During a very lonely moment, I decided to go for a long walk in the woods just beyond the farm. Once there, I stopped to take in the sights, sounds and smells of the sunny, crisp, fall day. Almost immediately, I felt a connection with the trees surrounding me, the earth below me, and the sky above me. Effortlessly, I found my mind settling down and the intensity of my loneliness easing up. I decided to just sit on a large boulder and enjoy the moment. Next thing I knew, I was enveloped in a web of natural peace, nature's gift to all of us.

---

[12] Matthew 5: 3

My loneliness vanished, entirely.

Then, a simple thought bubbled up into my awareness, emerging from some unknown depth within me, "Perhaps God wants me to experience a season of alones, so that a certain learning or growth can take shape within me." I can't say I never again had a bout with loneliness. What I can say, however, is that my loneliness had meaning and purpose— allowing me to endure it more gracefully.

In the context of God's wise, loving and purposeful will, the secret is to "resist nothing and accept everything." This is not an invitation to passivity or victimhood. Rather, it is an acknowledgment that God is present in all events and circumstances, most especially in our suffering. And if God is present, then the seeds of providence, redemption and resurrection are also present. Acceptance is the opposite of impulsive reactivity. Acceptance empowers us to stand back from fear, anxiety, and anger--giving us the space to breathe, to pray, and to listen to the voice of God. Thus, we don't react; we respond, with the wisdom and strength of heaven behind us.

On a lonely Saturday evening on the farm, I picked up a book to read—a biography of the life of Saint Francis of Assisi. A few pages into the book my loneliness gave way to curiosity. Francis was not born a saint. As a young man he chased women, enjoyed wild parties and fancied himself to be a conquering warrior. After a military failure, a stint in prison, and another military embarrassment, Francis surrendered his heart to God. Any loneliness I was experiencing gave way to inspired fascination, wonder and inspiration. I was sharing my evening with one of the world's greatest saints. From that moment forward Francis has walked with me--not as a historical figure but as a living, breathing presence, as my "spiritual father."

Francis was born to relatively wealthy parents in the year 1182; a lover of pleasure, he was known to indulge his appetites and to delight in displays of self-aggrandizement. When he could no longer satisfy his hunger for happiness through the fulfillment of the senses, Francis sought glory in the form of war. However, after a series of mishaps, he began to seek the fulfillment of interior longings in prayer and solitude.

A key moment in Francis' conversion took place while was praying before an ancient crucifix in the forsaken chapel of San Damiano, just outside of Assisi. Jesus spoke to him, "*In a tender voice.*" The message was clear and simple, "*Francis, repair my house, which is falling into ruins.*" Taking Jesus at his word, Francis began to repair old, abandoned churches in a spirit of love, joy and simplicity. His presence was so full of Divine energy that he began to attract followers. Soon, they embraced Francis' life of prayer, poverty and service. The following quote of a noted biographer of Francis perfectly captures the essence of his transformation:

"...this immense and unimaginably good God, Who addressed Francis in the form of the poor, crucified one, also brought him back to Life, gave him purpose, and rescued him from chaos.... Francis had Experienced God as author, renewer, and savior. He knew-in a way that was deeper and that surpassed all other modes of knowing-that God   saved him from turmoil and gave him meaning. Francis had not only been lifted from the depths of depression, he had been lifted from the prison of self. Henceforth his life would no longer be centered on himself, his needs, his past, his pleasure, his pain, his glory, his fulfillment. From this time forward, he had one goal in mind: to remain accessible to the voice that had just addressed him-to enable the conversion to continue."[13]

The entire spiritual life is simply a matter of remaining "accessible" to God's voice. To the extent that we are responsive to God's voice, our lives become God-like. Francis was so very accessible to Christ's voice that he became—in a manner of speaking—another Christ. To that point, two years before he died an angel appeared to Francis, piercing his hands, feet and side with a heavenly light. Henceforth, Francis bore the wounds of Christ—known as the stigmata --on his body for the remainder of his life. The lesson for all of us is that we become what we hear, what we attend to, what we obey, and what we love. Below is a brief description of Francis' stigmata experience written by one of his followers, Brother Angelo:

> "One morning two years before his death…while he was praying on the side of a mountain named La Verna, there appeared to him a seraph in the figure of a crucified man, having his hands and feet extended as though on a cross, and clearly showing the face of Jesus Christ. Two wings met above his head , two covered the rest of his body to the feet, and two were spread as in flight. When the vision passed, the soul of Francis was afire with love; and on his body there appeared the wonderful impression of the wounds of our Lord Jesus Christ."[14]

13: "The Reluctant Saint," Donald Spoto. Page 46.

14 Leg. 3. comp. 69.

3 The Process of Purification

**Jesus was led by the Spirit into the desert to be tempted.
- Gospel of Matthew**

The outer nature must undergo a change of poise, a purification. - Sri Aurobindo

To the degree that the first year with my foster family was difficult and challenging, the second year was both natural and easy. Acclimated to their routines and rhythms, I deeply enjoyed the love they offered me. Some of my most cherished memories include moments of working side-by-side with my foster father: bailing hay, repairing fences, cleaning septic systems, chasing animals, etc. He gave the orders and I dutifully obeyed. During these work fests, we seldom talked about anything of consequence. Yet, we enjoyed a deep, silent bond. I felt his strength, ingenuity and determined will—which helped me to feel safe and secure. More importantly, I was being given a glimpse into the real meaning of manhood. To this day, I draw on the energy and power inherent in these memories, and view them as precious gifts from God.

Now I was a senior in high school, and I had to choose a college and a course of study. I thought, prayed and deliberated about entering the seminary. Though I found the idea of being a priest powerfully attractive, I was not inclined towards celibacy, at all. I wanted to share my life with a woman. So I decided to major in both psychology and religious studies, determined to bridge secular and sacred worlds.

Eventually, I settled on a wonderful Franciscan college. During my time there I deepened my devotion to Francis, developed a love for learning, and uncovered a strong desire to spend my life serving God. Also, a romantic relationship begun in my senior year in high school blossomed into a steady, long term relationship. This is not the young woman my father asked me not to date, but a lady I met on a retreat. We married just weeks after graduating from College.

I'd like to say I followed Francis' example of remaining entirely "accessible" to God's voice, but I cannot. Shortly after marrying, we headed to the University of Notre Dame, so that I could study theology on the graduate level. I believed this would better prepare me for ministry. Over the next half-dozen years I would earn two graduate degrees, witness the birth of my two wonderful sons, work fulltime in Church Ministry, and enter into painful divorce proceedings.

A divorce induces suffering on many, many levels—impacting scores of people. One of the deeper levels of my own pain was a form of disillusionment with the Catholic Church, and perhaps God. My wife and I played by the rules: no premarital sex, no birth control, we devoted our lives to ministry, tithed, etc. And yet, our marriage ended in divorce.

Eventually, I came to see that our divorce was painfully inevitable. Though God's grace had elevated me out of many destructive patterns, some deep wounds remained. Simply put, I was not ready or able to enter fully into a marriage covenant. Sometimes, love is just not enough. This is not to say, paradoxically, that our marriage should not have happened. Beautiful children came from our union, and I learned much about myself. God's plans often exceed our ability to understand His ultimate purposes.

I came to realize that religious orthodoxy is not a guarantee against disappointment, loss or failure. At the time, however, I felt a needed to distance myself from anything overly Catholic. I stilled believed in God--with deist overtones. I prayed--at least a bit. And I still venerated Francis—though from a distance.

After my divorce, my professional life moved from ministry to counseling. I believed an "enlightened psychology" was the answer to human suffering. If I could just figure out why I did the stupid things I did, crack my neurotic code, learn to express my deepest pain, and stay in touch with my feelings at all times, my interior anguish would certainly morph into the joyful freedom of self-actualization. Subsequently, being "in touch" with myself became more important than being in touch with God and "feeling good" trumped doing good. In my attempt to "find myself," I was getting lost--in myself. The inevitable consequence of such a path was that my moral landscape became somewhat murky, and I found it increasingly easy to justify almost any of my actions.

It is not that I ceased to believe in God or became a moral degenerate. I simply considered myself to be among the intelligentsia—believing that Freud was as wise as Teresa of Avila, sociological research carried as much weight as scripture, and modern biblical scholars had as much insight into Jesus as did the saints. In short, I was an educated fool.

Throughout my adolescence there were many moments of legitimate illumination, times when God was palpable and real. However, illumination is not the end of the road. If we are sincere in our spiritual longings, illumination gives way to purification. It is naïve to think we can jump from flashes of enlightenment to a permanent state of God-union. I was in need of much purification.

Purification is not punishment. It is coming to terms with the fact that a civil war rages within us—replete with contrary desires, complex emotions, and powerful aversions. Sooner or later, our internal "demons" surface and take us for quite a ride. If there is any consolation in all of this, it is the fact that God understands the fear, confusion and pain underlying our foolishness. God is merciful. Lovingly, God uses our failures as a kind of pruning knife—purifying the sap of our interior life and causing our spirits to shoot upward and straighter. Thus, purification unfolds always within the scope of God's wise, compassionate and mysterious providence, and leads us ultimately to a place of supreme freedom.

Don't misunderstand me. Psychological insight has its place. Feelings need to be felt and trauma has to be processed. Yet, we cannot clean oil with oil—meaning that the most well informed mind is incapable of healing itself. Only a "higher" or "transcendent" or "elevated" consciousness can serve as a healing balm for the human spirit. Only a "power greater than ourselves can restore us to sanity." That "power" is the love, light and wisdom of God.

I was becoming acutely aware of the limits of psychotherapy when a moment of clarification came in the context of a supervision session with a wise and seasoned psychologist. I was presenting one of my more challenging cases to him when he made the following observation: "In my many years of being a psychologist, I have observed that those patients who heal and grow typically do so because they have found a spiritual path to follow. In opening their hearts to something bigger than themselves, they seem to find a way out of their suffering."

Given the immense respect I had for this man, his comment impacted me deeply. It gave me permission to return to my spiritual roots. Still, I was confused. I longed for the experience of God I had known in my adolescence. Yet, I knew I could not recreate the past. I did returned to Church, and certainly found a sense of God's presence in the Eucharist. My day-to-day life, however, was fraught with turmoil. Moods, emotions and a persistent sense of self-loathing were, at times, overwhelming. I was a tiny ship still being tossed about by the winds competing desires and confusing perspectives.

I did look to my Catholic world for direction, but found little or no help. At that time, the life of the American Catholic Church seemed to be divided along two distinct, competing paths: a rigid, doctrinaire approach to religion or an almost exclusive emphasis on social justice; neither paying much attention to the interior life. Yes, beliefs do matter and the Gospel commands us to generously care for the marginalized of society. But without the experience of what Jesus referred to as "living water," our beliefs and actions produce little or no fruit. Only the direct and immediate experience of God fulfills the deepest desires of the human heart. Otherwise, we are merely rearranging deck furniture on the Titanic. Without grace, today's oppressed often become tomorrow's oppressors.

Around this time, I had a very interesting and lucid dream: I was sitting in a room. Across from me was an unknown Yogi, wearing an orange robe. Between us was a table, and on the table was a picture of Jesus. I said to the Yogi, "I really want to follow you. I believe you can teach me to find God in such a way that my sense of His presence can be steady and unwavering. But I am a Christian and I can't turn my back on Jesus." The Yogi said nothing. He merely smiled at me. And the dream ended.

Shortly after my dream, I was introduced to a man who taught meditation and Yoga... I asked him if we could "discuss meditation?" Before he answered, he told me a few things about myself-- with uncanny accuracy. Then, he gave me his phone number and told me to give him a call. For close to a month. I called him almost daily. Finally, he returned my call. When I asked why it took him so long to return my call he replied, "I was testing you, to see if you were really interested in learning to meditate. I don't want to waste my time."

After being convinced of my sincerity, he agreed to become my meditation teacher. He made me promise to begin my day with a meditation practice. Of course, I agreed. Almost immediately, a level of peace and steadiness returned to my life. There was still internal pain, often intense, but my ability to watch it without being overshadowed by it began to grow. Again and again my teacher would tell me, "Don't identify with your past or the stories you have about yourself. You are never who you think you are."

His words began to ring true. I discovered that while I had a body, "I" was more than my body. I had emotions too, but "I" was larger than my emotions. And though I had a mind, "I" transcended my mind. This "I" was not the perseverating, self-obsessed critic that had haunted me most of my life, but a silent and spacious and compassionate witness to both the events of my life and the complexities of my mind. Spirituality became less and less about fixing the broken me and more and more about identifying with the "Self" or the "Soul" or what the Buddhists refer to as "The face we had before we were born."

Despite these flashes of liberation, something was still missing. There were still far too many periods of darkness or confusion. When I brought this to my meditation teacher's attention, he suggested that I consider taking his "guru" as my own guru—a living "Yogi" from India.[15] Given my loyalty to Christ, I could not or would not make this leap. Nevertheless, I maintained my meditation practice, and continued to experience moments of profound freedom and great upheaval.

Then one day, a dear colleague gave me a book and suggested that I read it. The book was titled, "Autobiography of a Yogi." It was written by a "Swami" from India, Paramahansa Yogananda.[16] I took the book home and began to read it. I was not prepared for what happened; it rocked my world. Though it is almost five-hundred pages, I read the entire book in two or three days, and then I read it again and again. At times, I would even sleep with the book. Finally, a real sense of clarity began to emerge.

To begin with, Yogananda believed that his mission to America was inspired by Jesus—because there were saints waiting to be awakened and not enough shepherds to awaken them. Secondly, the meditation practice and life-style he taught was completely adaptable to Christianity, and to any other traditional religious path. Thirdly, regardless if one is a monk or a householder, the absolute goal of life is to be a saint—defined not as a perfect person, but one who is stabilized in the experience of God-union. Fourthly, he stressed the essential importance of grace in the spiritual life. Lastly, Yogananda loved Saint Francis of Assisi. I was sold entirely, and continue to be!

---

[15] His guru's name was Yogi Bhajan, who brought Kundalini Yoga to the United states. He died in 2004.

[16] Paramahansa Yogananda came to the United States in 1920, and remained until his death in 1952. His autobiography is recognized as a spiritual classic.

With this clarification, however, came the realization that I was in need of a deeper level of purification. Though I had been faithful to my meditation practice and sought to ground my identity in God, I was still very inclined to do my own thing, chase my fancies, indulge my mind and call my own shots. Yogananda was very unambiguous in regard to this matter—the willingness to surrender one's life and will to God is an essential ingredient to the stabilized experience of God-union.

Growing up Catholic, Yogananda's challenge to surrender my life to the will of God was not unfamiliar. Yet in my theological sophistication, I had come to believe that such a simple, childlike approach to the spiritual life was no longer relevant. The complexities of modern life—so I believed--made God's will obtuse and difficult to discern, perhaps even outdated. I was intrigued, mystified and challenged by Yogananda's clarion call to surrender.

Early on in my discovery of Yogananda I had a dream that I believe was a visitation and a blessing from Yogananda. In the dream, I was escorted by two Indian men into a room where Yogananda was sitting. He nodded for me to speak. The very first thing I said was, "I apologize if I say something that is inappropriate. I have never spoken to someone of your stature." Yogananda smiled and again nodded for me to speak. I continued, "Will you take me on as a disciple? Because I believe you can take me all the way to God." Yogananda then reached out and placed his hand on my heart. A surge of energy or grace emanated from him and into me. I awoke from my sleep, feeling absolutely blissful.

Later that day, I attended a party at the house of a friend. One of his other guests—one that I had never met—apparently fancied herself as some sort of spiritual medium. She pulled me aside and said, "You have a powerful helper in heaven watching over you."

Rolling my eyes, I asked, "So who is this helper?"

She confidently answered, "Paramahansa Yogananda." I politely thanked her for the information and went home to meditate.

Make no mistake about it; surrendering to the will of God is not a call to servitude or religious legalism, but a call to love. The God of Jesus, Francis, Clare, Teresa, Therese, and Yogananda is a God of pure, unadulterated love. In surrendering to God, we are availing ourselves to the fulfillment of our heart's deepest desires—because God is a depthless font of goodness, wisdom, peace and joy. In the words of Francis of Assisi:

> "God, you are love, charity. You are wisdom. You are humility. You are patience. You are beauty. You are safety. You are rest. You are joy and gladness. You are hope. You are justice. You are temperance. You are all our treasure overflowing."[17]

We become what we focus on, what we give ourselves to, what we love. In loving God, our lives become more and more God-like, God-filled, and God-graced. Paradoxically, the call to surrender does not negate our freedom, but resurrects it from the muck and mire of confusion, fear and desire--liberating us to live creatively, intelligently, and compassionately.

Of course, surrender is not a destination, but a lifelong process. As I delved into Yogananda's writings, practiced his

---

17 This is exhortation, written by Francis, was given to Brother Leo and is preserved in the *SacroConvento* in Assisi, Italy

mediation techniques, and endeavored to implement his wisdom into my day-to-day life, my heart and consciousness began to heal and expand in positive ways—and continues to do so. God's grace operating in and through Yogananda did not rescue me from the process of purification, but enhanced my capacity for it.

Meditation became less about reducing stress or having a good experience, and more about God-union—not as an ecstatic escape from life, but as a deepening, interior silence. With this deepening silence, my compulsive mind and will became increasingly silent—silencing my desires and impulses and preoccupations. And from this place of silence, real contact with the spiritual world began to unfold—as wisdom, strength, inspiration, compassion, endurance, joy, peace and love. In other words, meditative silence is not the absence of thought, but the surrendering of our thought to God's thought—which is the force of love and truth.

One day, I was unfairly and severely criticized by a friend. Though I knew his barbs were unjustified, they still triggered a familiar level of painful self-doubt. I decided to meditate. After a period of time, a level of peace blanketed me. Then, a thought seemed to float down from above, directing me to seek the guidance of a wise and seasoned mentor—whose advice was absolutely helpful in dealing with this troubling matter. Over time, my thoughts, feelings, and imagination—began to be more and more organized around the intuitive experience of God's truth, beauty and goodness. There were fewer moments of darkness or self-hatred or terror. When those demons did arise, instead of obsessing or fleeing or raging, I learned to pray or meditate or simply surrender myself to God's care. Interestingly, the quickness of heaven's response seemed proportionate to the sincerity of my prayer.

Again, I cannot state emphatically enough that my discovery of Yogananda and the practice of Kriya Yoga did not take me out of the purification process, but deepened my capacity for it. There were times—and still are—when the pain that arose from within me was virtually unbearable. Sometimes it felt as though a sword was piercing my heart. In the past, I would have fled such experiences, but somehow God's grace gave me the capacity to stand fast, to trust, and to prayerfully stay present. After coming out of these experiences, my heart always felt more open and my awareness more expanded and my spirit more supple.

Francis' emphasis on poverty took on a whole new meaning. Being a married person with financial responsibilities, I could not live a life of literal poverty. However, I was clearly being called to a life of spiritual or interior poverty. This meant that I could no longer rely on my own cleverness, my own strength, or my own abilities. I had to rely entirely on God, and the grace that flowed through Jesus, and Francis and Yogananda. I began to realize that I was nothing, and God was everything—which was actually very liberating. The only thing that made sense to me was God's will, even if I did not understand it. Increasingly, I prayed only to be aligned to God's will.

During a conversation with my meditation teacher, I was confronted with God's will. I mentioned that I had an upcoming date with a young, beautiful woman—intonating, with pride, that I was hoping to get "lucky." Though he said nothing, his silence spoke volumes. So I asked, "What's up?"

He answered, "When you make love to a woman you leave an imprint on her soul."

"What are you saying?"

"I am saying that leaving an imprint on someone's soul is a huge responsibility."

"Are you saying that I should not have sex with her?"

Taking a slow, deep breath, He replied, "I'm saying don't write a check with your body that your life can't cash."

"You sound very Catholic."

"Truth is truth, regardless of the source."

"It feels like you are channeling God's will for me in this matter."

"The truth is always God's will."

I must say, however, that in these periods of deep purification there were also many profound graces. I often experienced—and still do—hidden hands carrying me, supporting me, and loving me. Literally, I experienced Yogananda's hand on my life, and still do. The right people would come to me with the right answers, the right words and the right wisdom. At every turn, I found myself at God's wonderful mercy, which is the only way to really live. To the degree that our human will is aligned with the Divine will, the forces of nature naturally support our endeavors.

The purification process is, of course, ongoing. But the fruits were beginning to blossom forth. My mind was being resurrected from ignorance, my heart resurrected from fear and my will resurrected from compulsion. Along with this process of resurrection came a sense of freedom, not to do whatever I wanted, but to increasingly give myself over to God's truth, beauty and goodness. My life was not about me, and never was. What I began to discover was that the pinnacle of human intelligence and creativity and freedom is not self-assertion or self-actualization, but the experience of being an instrument of God's love, period.

Jesus' temptations in the desert--over a forty day period—capture perfectly the purification experience. Though he was "whole" and "complete" and without "sin," he was led by God into the process of purification. We are told in Mark's Gospel that "The Spirit drove him out into the wilderness. And he was in the wilderness for forty day, tempted by Satan."[18] As the "New Adam," Jesus had to confront, resist, and transcend the primordial temptations common to the human race, not for him, but for all of us. His purification ordeal, however, was not merely a modeling process. He was doing more than showing us how to do it. In saying "no" to the darker tendencies in human nature and "yes" to our highest and noblest possibilities, more grace and power and light were unleashed into the human arena. This is made clear at the end of Jesus' purification ordeal when we are told, "...the devil left him, and behold angels came and ministered to him."[19]

People ask me if I believe in hell. They are always surprised when I reply in the affirmative. I go on to explain, however, that hell is not a place, but a state of consciousness. We are in hell whenever we feel "distant" or 'separate" or "cutoff" from God. The fact of the matter is that we can't really be away from God, because God is very ground of our existence. If God were not with us or in us, we would cease to exist. We "feel" as though we are in hell when we are locked inside of our distorted thoughts and our disfigured emotions, and are unable to hear or see or feel God's truth, beauty and goodness. Hell is nothing other than the prison of absolute, radical subjectivity—being lost and isolated within our interior perceptions of reality. Furthermore, when we are mired in painful subjectivity, does it not feel like eternity?

---

[18] Matthew: 4:1

[19] Matthew: 4:11

"Hell is the state of the soul powerless to come out of itself, absolute self-centeredness, dark and evil isolation, i.e., final inability to love."[20]

My purification process brought me to a challenging but liberating realization: my personal hell would continue to the degree that I elevated my will over and against God's will. Implied in this realization is the fact that God's will is both knowable and accessible—as "Truth" born of Divine "Love."

The "Good News" is that the portal into God's "power" or "grace" or "light" is wide open. Through the pain we suffer and the glimpses of joy that we experience, God is calling us home—into deeper and deeper states of God-communion. What is required is not perfection, but a childlike act of faith—offered again and again: a simple "yes" to God's ever-present presence, the lifting of our hearts and minds towards heaven, and the willingness to do God's will. Such acts of faith draw the forces of heaven to us. Jesus said, "There is more joy in heaven over one sinner who repents than over ninety-nine righteous persons who need no repentance."[21]

I shared my story of purification—which is ongoing-- not because I am unique or special or holy, but to bear witness to God's wondrous, merciful love. God's saints are waiting to take us by the hand and lead us home--to our ultimate destiny. Yes, the journey to heaven will take us through hell, but not the hell of damnation, but of purification. It is the most exciting, meaningful, challenging and fulfilling journey that a man or woman can take. It humanizes and divinizes us--all at the same time. It is the ultimate love affair!

---

[20] Nicolas Berdyaev, The Destiny of Man, London, 1937, pg. 351.

[21] Luke: 15:7

I will close this chapter with a story from the life of Francis of Assisi. It captures perfectly the challenge and joy and freedom of Francis' journey of purification—and of our own. Enjoy!

"One day he was carrying stones down the hill from Assisi, when a leper was approaching him on the trail. There was no way to avoid him. Francis was nervous. He did not want to put down the stone and give the leper something. Francis did not want to encounter the leper at all. There was no way to avoid the man approaching in torn clothes and open sores on his face and body.

What was only seconds felt like forever. Francis was about to turn his head and look away as he always had done before, he found his attention fixed on the leper. He was not so ugly. He studied the young man.... The leper was surprisingly quite beautiful. He was a human being. Each sore on his body was full of a story. His eyes were sunken, but not defeated. Francis glanced at the palms of his hands which looked gentle, soft, vulnerable. As the leper was climbing the hill, Francis found himself turned around, still drinking in the details of their encounter.

His whole life, he had always turned his head from anything remotely disturbing. These things that were actually people did not exist, at least not for Francis. Today, something stopped this automatic response and he dared to look. This leper was a man. He had a soul. Before Francis knew it, he had dropped his stones and ran back up the hill toward the stranger. Surprised, the leper turned and looked at him. Francis did not know what to say. His arms began to gesture their mutual helplessness when Francis found himself moving towards the leper, reaching for his face, yes kissing him on the lips. This man in that moment was God. And God was freeing Francis.

As Francis stood back, the leper smiled from cheek to cheek. He slowly turned and continued along his way. For Francis, everything ugly was now and forever a part of God's beauty. The leper was a man. He was not just another leper. Francis would never see illness and poverty, suffering and death the same again. His heart had only to look once and see what is really present. How can nakedness be anything but holy?"[22]

---

22 "Simple Peace: The Spiritual Life of Saint Francis of Assisi." Bruce Davis, Ph.D.

Page 8-9

4 KRIYA YOGA: THE PATH OF SILENCE AND SURRENDER

To forget God is to miss the whole point of existence. Learn to feel God and enjoy Him. - Yogananda

"Seek first the kingdom of God and its righteousness, and everything else you need shall be added unto you." - Jesus

The path of Kriya Yoga as taught by Yogananda is breathtakingly simple. The purpose of life is not to find a soul mate, create wealth or develop the perfect body, but to love God and then extend that love to more and more people. Loving God, however, is neither an intellectual affair nor a sentimental state of mind. It is the experience of "oneness" or "union" with God. The word "kriya" means "action" and "yoga" means "union." Thus, Kriya Yoga is founded on time-tested actions that lead a person to the experience of union with God—centered on a specific meditation practice, a balanced lifestyle and right living.

Given the fact that the meditation technique associated with

47

Kriya Yoga can only be taught by an authorized teacher, and within the context of an initiation ceremony, I was formally initiated by one of Yogananda's direct disciples.[23] Part and parcel of the initiation ceremony is a "commitment" or "promise" to meditate daily. While the benefits of the Kriya meditation practice include reduced stress and better mental functioning, the real goal is God-union. And God-union is realized in and through the ever-deepening experience of the "Great Silence."[24]

Before delving into the theme of the "Great Silence," it would be helpful to explain what my initiation into Kriya Yoga represented--being much more than a promise to meditate or a pleasant ritual. It was, in fact, the beginning of an entirely new life.

Prior to my discovery of Kriya Yoga, I certainly loved God; but I loved my own desires, impulses and appetites more. My spirituality was an attempt to accommodate God's will to my own. I did experience an occasional "tryst" with God; they were, however, more like a series of one night stands rather that a spiritual marriage. There were moments of "quiet" and "peace" and "presence," but they were easily lost in the onslaught of my restless desiring.

For me, initiation into Kriya Yoga was a betrothal of sorts— to God. I had experienced a taste of what Teresa of Avila referred to as the "Prayer of union;"[1] and I longed to have my

---

23 At the Kriya initiation the primary meditative technique is taught, and a blessing is given—through which God's grace is bestowed on the person receiving initiation. Initiation can only be given by one authorized to do so.

24 The "prayer of union" is a grace given by God whereby the faculties of the mind—imagination, desire and thinking—are shut down and what remains is a state of silent, pure union with God.

life stabilized against the backdrop of that "union." In short, my initiation into Kriya Yoga was the beginning of an ongoing process of surrendering my life to God, entirely—of making my heart and soul entirely accessible to God's voice.

On a practical level, I began every day with meditation—often for two hours at a sitting. I stayed away from situations that were fraught with chaos and confusion. Though innately extraverted, I cultivated a liking for solitude. My spiritual reading centered on books written by saints and recognized sages; and I attempted to use more of my discretionary time in the service of others—even taking a part-time job as "pastoral administrator" in an inner-city church.

Please understand that I am describing, in summary form, a process that took place over time; and is still ongoing. Also, I do not want to gives the impression that I became a hermit. I had and have a full caseload of psychotherapy clients, I enjoyed and still enjoy my family, and I remain a steadfast fan of the New York Yankees. The difference is that I attempt to contextualized my activities, sometimes successfully and sometimes not, against the backdrop of my spiritual path.

A poignant moment took place sometime after my initiation, capturing perfectly the ongoing process of spiritual surrender. On a warm July night, I was enjoying a quiet cup of coffee at an outdoor café, when an absolutely gorgeous young woman sat at the table next to me. At first we merely nodded to each other; the nod was followed a "hello," which then led to a two-hour animated conversation about politics, psychology and spirituality. At the conclusion of our discussion, she stated, "I have something very strange to say to you."

To which I answered, "God ahead. Just say it."

"I think you and I are going to married someday. I just feel it. I don't typically do this, at all. But I would like you to come home with me tonight."

I swallowed hard, and said, "Don't go anywhere. I have to go to the bathroom."

I did not have to go to the bathroom. I just needed some space to think, and to pray. I did not know what to do. So, I prayed, "God, Christ and Yogananda, what do you want me to do?"

What came to me, immediately, was a story about the Buddha. Just prior to his "Enlightenment" experience, he was tempted by a demon with a vision of beautiful women trying to seduce him. Of course, the Buddha resisted the temptation; and shortly thereafter he attained enlightenment.

For me, the message was clear. Part of me wanted to say "Yes," but the wiser part of "me" knew that this was some kind of test; and that a new threshold of freedom was waiting just beyond it. So, I went outside; took a deep breath, and said "No thank you."

She asked if I was "*gay*" or had a "girlfriend" or if my "plumbing was in working order."

I tried to explain that it was a "spiritual thing" and that she was "quite beautiful" and that I was "flattered" by her offer, but the answer was "no." We shook hands, parted and never had contact after that evening.

I wish I could say, in keeping with the Buddha's story that enlightenment descended upon me. However, no such thing took place. But, two blessings did come my way. I made a decision to be celibate, until or unless God blessed me with a wife—celibacy was not always easy, but it certainly simplified my life and my spiritual path. Secondly, a few days per month I had consistently experienced intense feelings of lust, that took all of my power to control—at times, unsuccessfully. After saying "No" to this young woman, the bouts of intense lust never returned. What remained was a normal, healthy sex drive. It was as if an "exorcism" had taken pace.

I don't want you to think that the ultimate goal of a passionately intense spiritual life is some form of stoic self-denial. Nothing could be further from the truth. Love of God, experienced as unfettered union, is the beginning and the end of the spiritual life. Once you have had a taste of this loving union, you necessarily and naturally want to orient your life to union—with God. Parents, for example, make many sacrifices for their children—not out of legalistic duty, but out of love for their children. It is the very same process with God; only on much more heightened or elevated level.

Thus, the change that begun with my initiation into Kriya Yoga was a simple but profound redirecting of my attention, will and energy towards God's presence—most often experienced as peace, stillness, and silence. Instead of trying to make God orbit around my whims, the goal is to center my life around God's will—bubbling up from the "Great Silence."

It might be helpful to situate the theme of "silence" in the context of a cherished aspect of the Catholic ethos. I fondly remember my best friend and myself marching off to church on a Saturday afternoon for the expressed purpose of going to confession. As fast as our mouths might have been moving before we entered the church, they would automatically close upon entering God's house. Before going in to the confessional, we would kneel in silence, reflecting on the sins we were about to confess--and deciding which ones we should keep to ourselves.

Then, there was the ritual of standing in the confessional line, in silence. Once in the confessional box, we typically would wait--in silence--for the person on the other side to finish their confession. When it was our turn, we would whisper our sins to the priest and he would then give us absolution in hushed tones, unless we deserved a good tongue lashing, which seemed to happen to me fairly often. Finally, we prayed our penitential prayers in silence. Silence was the contextual norm for the experience of God--the portal through which we entered into the mystery of God's presence.

The "Great Silence" is not the absence of noise or mere quiet or the process of stilling the mind. It is God's pure, untainted presence breaking into our awareness. It is the direct and immediate experience of the Divine, beyond the mediation of thoughts, words or concepts. It is God's simple, blissful and uncomplicated presence. Remember the words of the Psalmist, "Be still and know that I am God."[25]

We can't make the "Great Silence" happen because we cannot control God. It comes as gift, as grace, and as favor. Yet, we can be confident that God desires us to experience His unspeakable Presence. In the words of Sri Aurobindo:

> "Silence is a state of consciousness which comes of itself from above when you open to the Divine Consciousness. Silence is the condition of being when it returns to the Divine."[26]

The hallmark of a vast majority of meditation practices is the use of a mantra, most often the loving, prayerful repetition of "God's Name." In the Kriya Yoga tradition, the use of a

---

[25] Psalm 46:10

[26] M.P. Pandit, Dictionary of Sri Aurobindo's Yoga, page 233

mantra is often combined with the gentle process of regulating breath and redistributing the "life force," so as to deepen our attunement to the Great Silence. Whatever the specific technique might be, what is most important is the heartfelt stance of a simple, open longing for the Divine Beloved. To once again quote Sri Aurobindo:

> "It is easier to let the Silence descend into you...to open yourself and let it descend...to remain quiet at the time of meditation, not fighting with the mind or making mental efforts to pull down the silence or the Power, but keeping only a silent will and aspiration for them." [27]

One of my first experiences of the Great Silence occurred indirectly, when I was an adolescent living in a rectory full of priests. I was approaching the Pastor's office to ask him a question, when I was stopped dead in my tracks. Literally, I experienced a wall of peaceful energy at the entrance to his office. Taking a deep breath and crossing this mysterious threshold, I walked in. What I saw astounded me. The Pastor was on his knees, silently praying, oblivious to my presence, and apparently absorbed in God. More importantly, there was a palpable but indescribable presence in room—silent, deep and enveloping; yes, God's Presence. I did not want to speak and I did not want to leave. Feeling a bit voyeuristic, I eventually tip-toed out of the room, unnoticed. However, a certain "afterglow" remained with me for a number of days—a clear and discernible sense of peace.

Putting the experience of the Great Silence in more poetic terms is the following quote from Thomas Merton:

> "Where is silence? Where is solitude? Where is love? For religion goes beyond words and actions, and attains to

---

[27] Ibid, page 234

the ultimate truth only in silence and Love...Ultimately these cannot be found anywhere except in the ground of our own being. There, in the silent depths, there is no more distinction between the I and the Not-I. There is perfect peace, because we are grounded in infinite creative and redemptive love...Only in silence and solitude, in the quiet of worship, the reverent peace of prayer, the adoration in which the entire ego-self silences and abases itself in the presence of the Indivisible God to receive His one Word of Love; only in these "activities" which are "non-actions" does the spirit truly wake from the dream of multifarious, confused, and agitated existence."[28]

If people are going to live a full spiritual life—Christian or otherwise—meditative silence is not an option, but a necessity. In many quarters, Christianity is reduced to "kindness" or "justice" or "treating others as you want to be treated." These virtues are certainly noble and good, but they are the fruits of the spiritual life, not the essence. When asked about the heart and soul of his religion, Jesus replied,

"You shall love the Lord your God with all your heart, and with all your soul, and with all your mind. This is the great and first commandment. And the second is like it, you shall love your neighbor as yourself. On these two commandments depend all the law and the prophets."[29]

Often, people blithely reduce Jesus' primary teaching to "loving others." However, the priority and sequence of Jesus' words give us a very different message. Loving God with our entire being is the precondition for loving others. The

---

[28] This is an excerpt from Merton's essay, "Love and Solitude," LL 20-24.

[29] Matthew 23:37-40

Apostle John tells us that "God is love."[30] We can only love others to the extent that we experience union with God— Who is Love. Our capacity to love God is always the fruit of our love for God. In reality, there are not many loves, but one love--God. When we authentically love others, we are simply allowing God's intelligence, energy and grace to flow through us—as a momentum of unity. God is love. We become "one with others" to the extent that we realize our oneness with God. The following quote from Yogananda perfectly captures this truth:

> "Always remember: your heavenly Father loves you unconditionally.... I have realized that it was someone Else who cared for me through all the human loves. The Divine has loved me as mother, as father, and as friends... God is behind everything."[31]

Before we can love others or live a virtuous life, we must first love God. Loving God is uniting with God—as the Great Silence, in and through prayerful meditation. A humorous story might convey this truth. One night when my sons were teenagers, I was in a particularly annoyed state of my mind. After a sharp response from me to one of their questions, they both asked, "Dad, did you meditate today?"

My response was "No."

"They replied, in unison, "Don't you think you should?" Dutifully, I meditated. They were happier, and so was I.

––––––––––––––––

[30] 1 John 4-8

[31] This quote from Yogananda was recited during at talk given by one of his direct disciples. I wrote the quote down, but I don't know exactly what the written source may have been.

Prior to my initiation into Kriya Yoga, it would have been accurate to say that I was in love with my own thinking-ness—meaning that I tended to be obsessed with my own thoughts, interpretations, and opinions. The more I entered into God's silent presence, however, the more I realized that the vast majority of my thoughts were nothing more than habitual, recycled concepts--without any fresh insight or intelligence or inspiration. By contrast, thoughts that arise from the Great Silence always carry the scent of truth, goodness, clarity, peace, compassion, strength and grace—serving the spiritual evolution of everyone involved.

When I find myself in a confusing or perplexing situation, I am learning to stop, to breathe and to ask for guidance—often praying to be an instrument of God's peace. Sooner or later, inspiration flows in the form of an intuition, common sense or a word of wisdom from a friend. I am discovering that our minds have been created so as to be instruments of God's wisdom or intelligence; and that meditation and prayer are the means by which we avail ourselves to heavenly inspiration.

God's silent presence calms the mind, gives rest to the nervous system, and softens the heart. This makes it very difficult for compulsive thoughts, destructive desires and addictive patterns to incubate—allowing our spirits to become more suppler, more pliable, and more yielding. Thus, God's thoughts begin to bubble up into our awareness. God's impulses begin to inspire our will. God's heart begins to love through our hearts. Our lives are directed by God's wisdom, power and grace—even concerning the most mundane aspects of our daily existence. Yes, nurturing our conscious contact with the Great Silence is most practical thing we could ever do!

The ultimate goal of mediation is to carry the awareness of

God's presence into our day-to-day lives. Hence, the Apostle Paul tells us to "Pray unceasingly."[32] Kriya Yoga has not caused me to be lost in spiritual ecstasy, but to faithfully and wisely discharge my responsibilities—while never forgetting God, not even for a moment. While my physical eyes engage the world, I attempt to keep the eye of the soul fixed on God.

I am not talking about a dreamy or otherworldly trance, but a moment by moment awareness of God's presence--manifesting as gentle alertness, inner calmness, and loving expansiveness. The body feels pain, the emotions register discomfort and the reactive mind spews its chatter, but our interior spirit remains tethered to the thought or image or sense of God. This is teaching me to respond rather than react, to seek the scent of God's wisdom, to draw upon the very same "intelligence" that guided Jesus—allowing God's genius to flow through me.

A practical example of this occurred when my youngest son was a senior in High School. Our country was on the verge of going to war with Iraq for the second time and there were major protests planned in New York City, which was about a six hour car ride from where we lived. My son wanted to attend the upcoming protests with a group of his friends. When I inquired as to whether or not there would be chaperones, he boldly responded, "No! We don't need them."

To which I responded, "Well then, you can't go."

He then put his hands on his hips—displaying a posture of authority—and replied, "This is a matter of conscience. I am going!"

---

[32] Ephesians 6:18

Adrenaline surged through my body and my face became red with anger. My first impulse to jack him up against the wall, and challenge him to push me out of the way. Given the fact that I was twice his size, I was sure I'd win that battle. Thankfully, there was a deeper, more discerning response within me. My son was a really sweet young man and we had a great relationship. Yet, my parental intuition said that going to New York City was not a good idea.

So I prayed—on the spot—internally, asking for guidance. And the following words effortlessly and calmly flowed from my mouth, "Very well. But know that if you no longer choose to accept my authority, you will no longer get my discretionary money. This means that I will no longer pay for any of your music lessons now or when you are in college." Immediately he answered, "That's not fair." To which I reiterated, "If you don't accept my authority, you don't get my discretionary money. I think that is very fair." His friends did go to New York, without him. A week or so later he told me, "You made me really angry, but I knew what you said made sense. I knew it was fair. So I chose not to go."

Staying tethered to God in the midst of our daily activities is not necessarily easy. It requires a level of "vigilance" or "wakefulness," as well as a certain interiority or reserve—keeping a portion of our spirit only for God and ourselves. Kriya Yoga has challenged me to remain present and prayerful, in both pleasant and unpleasant circumstances. At first, it takes a great deal of effort. But over time, it becomes natural and effortless. The following quote is from a great Indian saint, Anandamayi Ma. Her sage advice is both relevant and universal:

> "Choose a word, a form, an image, a symbol—in fact anything representing Him as a whole or in part—and, whether in happiness or misery, ceaselessly direct the current of your thinking towards it. Even though the

mind may repeatedly wander here or there, it will again seek rest in this center. In due course, love and devotion will awaken for Him who will then take possession of your heart."[33]

By now, I hope you can begin to appreciate the paradoxical nature of the Great Silence. It brings us into stillness, into peace, and into communion with God, but it also can propel our lives in directions we never imagined or would otherwise choose. Thus, an infallibly sure sign that a person is in contact with God is peace, humility, and a greater capacity for self-less service.

My life seemed to be going along just fine. My daily meditation routine was taking me deeper and deeper into the Great Silence. My psychotherapy practice was solid. And I was working as a part-time Pastoral Administrator at a local parish—even sharing the preaching load with the priest. However, a degree of discontent began to grow within me in reference to my position within the parish. It no longer felt "right." There was something else I felt called to, but had no idea of what it was. After prayerful discernment and consultations with trusted advisors, I offered my resignation to the Bishop.

Coinciding with my resignation, I attended a week long retreat with one of Yogananda's direct disciples, the same individual who had initiated me into Kriya Yoga. While on the retreat, an elderly gentleman continuously and forcefully encouraged me to ask for permission to teach Kriya Yoga. I repeatedly replied, "No, I am not ready or worthy to do such a thing." But he persisted. Just to get him off my back, I agreed to meet with Yogananda's disciple.

---

[33] "Women of Power and Grace," "The Wake Up Press," Santa Barbara,

It was a bit like going to the principal's office. I was nervous and a bit flustered. His gentle demeanor, however, immediately put me at ease. In fact, for the first ten minutes we discussed weight lifting and body building. Finally, I asked him if I could teach Kriya Yoga, in the distant future of course. He looked at me with a discerning eye, while becoming very silent. After a moment or two, he simply said, "Yes." I asked, "When?"

"Now" he replied. He gave me some instructions and off I went.

Five months later—on October 4th, the feast day of Francis of Assisi—we held of our first Kriya Yoga meditation service, in a meeting room adjacent to my counseling office. Besides myself, just four other people showed up, and even though I did not know what I was doing, the four people returned the following week—bringing some of their friends. We kept on meeting, week after week.

Soon, we outgrew the room we had been using. We rented a larger space within the same building and set it up as a meditation temple. We started offering retreats, classes, pilgrimages, and other programs. There were, of course, problems and challenges, but through it all we continued to grow. Eventually, we formed a "Board of Directors" and became a not-for-profit corporation.

We chose the "Assisi Institute" as our official name—because of Yogananda's great reverence for Francis, because of my devotion to Francis and because Francis is seen as a universal saint--honored by many different traditions and is the perfect bridge for the marriage of Eastern and Western spirituality. Among our members are Catholics, Protestants, Jews, Hindus, Buddhists, etc. We are not a Church in the formal sense, but a spiritual community. We do not hold Sunday services and members are encouraged to stay connected to their religious roots.

In this context, a number of things stand out to me in reference to our growth. First of all, people of all traditions are hungry for a contemplative spirituality—one that takes them into the Great Silence. They want to experience God directly and immediately. And they are willing to make a commitment to a daily meditation practice--and to alter their lifestyles when needed. Secondly, I sincerely believe our mission is guided from above--by the grace of Jesus, Francis and most especially Yogananda. We do what we do because of God's grace. We are dependent on heavenly wisdom and not our own cleverness. We are a very imperfect community of people, but we do love God and desire to serve those that are sent our way.

Our mission is essentially Yogananda's mission: "To reestablish God in the temple of souls through revival of the original teachings of God-communion as propounded by Christ and Krishna...."[34] While the world's religions differ theologically, their mystical traditions seem to follow the same map—often referred to as the "Perennial Philosophy." For example, when the mystical traditions of Christianity, Judaism, and Hinduism are placed side by side, it is clear that they are describing the same experiences—albeit in different cultural garbs. Without a doubt, we are drinking from the same well, drawing upon the same grace, and entering into the one, indivisible Presence—in and through the Great Silence.

Our work at the Assisi Institute is not to convert Christians to Hinduism, Hindus to Buddhism, or Buddhists to Islam, or Muslims to Judaism. Rather, we teach people to meditate, to

---

[34] Paramahansa Yogananda: *"The Second Coming of Christ,"* page xxviii

deepen their interior silence, to follow the Ten Commandments, to attune their lives to God's will, to lovingly serve others, to cultivate simplicity and humility, to nurture joy and to live a contemplative life in the world. And by our prayer, meditation and silence, we are endeavoring to become a community of love—indeed, a vortex of hallowed and sacred silence.

On a more personal note, my practice of Kriya Yoga has not taken me away from Christianity—at all. Just as the "wise men from the East" placed gifts at the feet of the young Jesus, Yogananda has brought me back to Christ's feet—and is teaching me to me drink from the spring of Christ's own consciousness. Yes, my Christian and Catholic genes are functioning quite well. I must admit, however, that I also have Jewish genes, Hindu genes, Sufi Muslim genes, Buddhist's genes, Native American genes, etc. Given the fact that we have all arisen for the same "Divine Logos or Mind or Genius," I suspect we all share the same spiritual genes; we just don't know it yet.

It might be helpful to close this chapter with a reflection on the life of Francis of Assisi. Francis is often honored for his commitment to the poor, accurately so. But what often goes unmentioned was his commitment to contemplation, solitude and silence. Yes! Francis served the poor, but he spent an equal amount of time—perhaps even more time—in prayerful communion with God. We are told that when left alone, "He would fill the groves with sighs, sprinkle the ground with tears, strike his breast with his fist and, having found there a secret hiding place, converse with his Lord."[35] Francis drew his strength, his clarity and his love from Christ

---

[35] Saint Bonaventure: *"The Life of Francis,"* pg. 107.

and the Great Silence. The following reflection written by his biographer, Saint Bonaventure, perfectly captures Francis' love of prayer, silence and God-communion:

"Realizing that while he was in the body he was exiled from the Lord, since he was made totally insensible to earthly desires through his love of Christ, the servant of Christ strove to keep his spirit in the presence of God, by prayer without ceasing so that he might not be without the comfort of his beloved. Prayer was a delight to this contemplative who had already become a fellow citizen of the angels and who, making the rounds of heavenly mansions, sought with burning desire that Beloved from whom he was separated only by a wall of the flesh. Prayer was a support to this worker; for in everything which he did, distrusting his own effort and trusting God's loving concern, he casts his care completely upon the Lord in urgent prayers to him. He used to state firmly that the grace of prayer was to be desired above all else...believing that without it no one could prosper in God's service.... For whether walking or sitting, inside or outside, working or resting, he was so intent on prayer that he seemed to have dedicated to it not only his heart and body, but also all his effort and time."[36]

---

[36] Ibid: pg. 105

My spiritual Father, Richard Rohr

This is Yogananda's guru Sri Yukteswar, who many years ago wrote a book, "The Holy Science" which showed the underlying unity between Hinduism and Christianity

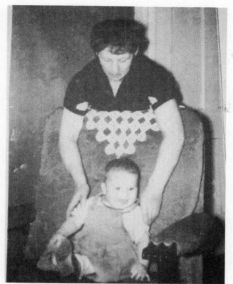

My mother and myself

This photo of Yogananda was taken minutes before he left his body. He knew that his death was imminent; he was staring into eternity-a final blessing for his followers

This portrait by Cimabue can be found in the Cathedral of St. Francis in Assisi, Italy. It is considered to be the closest likeness of St. Francis because Cimabue's painting was guided by friars who personally knew Francis

This photo was taken in Assisi Italy, at the conclusion of our marriage ceremony. One of the most beautiful days of my entire life

My dear Spiritual Brother, Swami Nirvanananda

A portion of the Assisi Institute Building

My wonderful foster parents, Tom and Jean Cass. My foster father happens to be an ordained deacon in the Catholic Church

This is a photo taken approximately a month after I moved in with my foster family, I was sixteen years of age

A younger version of myself with my son Nicholas

And with my son Michael

From left to right: my stepson Evan, my step daughter Alana, my son Nick and his wife Meredith, my son Michael's girlfriend Erin, my son Michael and my step daughter Tori

Paramahansa Yogananda stated that Jesus came to him for the purpose of blessing his mission in the West. He said this painting closely resembles what Jesus actually looked like

5 SELF-REALIZATION: DISCOVERING OUR IDENTITY IN GOD

But go to my brethren and tell them I am ascending to my Father and your Father.   - Jesus

Let us make mankind in our image, after our likeness. - Genesis

The world's scriptures declare man to be not a corruptible body, but a living soul. - Yogananda

While in the sixth grade, another student and I were engaged in what the good sisters referred to as "fisticuffs." Yes, we were fighting—which was not an entirely new experience for either of us. Before too much damage could be done, the fight was broken up and we were hauled into the school office. We were separated, I was sent to Sister Minelpha's room. Looking more disappointed than angry, she began to address me:

"You bold hunk of humanity, what in God's name is wrong with you?"

Staring at the floor, I replied, "I don't know,"

"You just can't get out of your own way. Can you?"

Hating to disappoint her, I answered, "I am sorry Sister."

Grabbing my chin and forcing me to have eye contact with her, "Who are you?"

Bewildered and thinking her advanced age had finally caught up with her, I answered, "I'm Craig. You know. I'm one of your students.

"Don't be stupid. I know your name. I mean that you don't know who you really are. You don't know that you are God's child, made in His image and likeness. And until you know that in your bones, you are going to keep getting yourself into trouble."

I had no idea what she was talking about. I only knew tears were filling my eyes. "Am I going to be punished Sister?"

"Of course you are, after school."

My punishment that day was one I have never forgotten. Sister took me to the Church. Together we prayed the rosary, the joyful mysteries to be exact. By the end of our time together, a palpable serenity settled on both of us. What a wise woman she was. She knew I was agitated, confused and feeling horrible about myself. Rather than focusing on the symptoms, she took me to the very font of wellness and wholeness. She brought me to God, and in the light of God's presence, I momentarily caught a glimpse of my true self--a living, breathing child of God!

Prior to my practice of Kriya Yoga, I was obsessed with

healing my psyche and finding personal happiness--all in the name of God, of course. I had forgotten the truth of Sister Minelpha's words, *"You are God's child, made in His image and likeness."* Instead, I was trying to construct a self-actualized personality, one that would do Sigmund Freud proud. Then, I read the words of Yogananda:

"Identifying himself with a shallow ego, man takes for granted that it is he who thinks, wills, feels, digests meals, and keeps himself alive. Never admitting that in his ordinary life he is naught but a puppet of past actions (karma) and of nature or environment. Each man's intellectual reactions, feelings, moods, and habits are merely the result of past actions... Lofty above such influences, however, is his regal soul. Spurning the transitory truths and freedoms, the Kriya Yogi passes beyond all disillusionment into his unfettered Being. The world's scriptures declare man not to be a corruptible body but a living soul." [37]

Simply put, my attention shifted from a preoccupation with my personality to practicing the presence of God, and to the truth of my identity in God. Specifically, I have a personality, but I am not my personality. I am the very "image and likeness" of God. I do not have a soul; I am soul. And the soul is prior to and larger than my psychological conditioning.

The practical fruit of this realization is that instead of viewing my wounds as a curse, I began to see them as openings to a world beyond self-preoccupation—exposing me to an infinite field of Divine presence and my actual identity in God. Now, instead of spending endless hours and enormous levels of energy analyzing the causes of my psychological pain, I carry it prayerfully and gracefully—surrendering myself to God.

---

37 *Autobiography of a Yogi,"* Paramahansa Yogananda:: Self-Realization Fellowship, Thirteenth Edition, pg. 243

On one occasion, for example, the Assisi Institute was hosting an interfaith prayer service--with representatives of all the major faith traditions taking part in it. My job was to host the event, while also presenting some closing remarks. A few hours before the service began, I was flooded with painful feelings of inadequacy and shame. Instead of becoming trapped within my emotional misery, I consciously breathed, pulled my awareness to my "third eye" and began to repeat the "Jesus Prayer." I continued this practice for about an hour, while running errands and preparing for the prayer service. Two things occurred as a result: I was able to stand back and compassionately witness my pain, and eventually, the pain disappeared altogether. This kind of spiritual vigilance is a way of life.

Putting it in a biblical context, in the Genesis story of creation it is implied that Adam and Eve walked with God "...in the cool of the day."[38] This indicates that they experienced a living, breathing intimacy with God. Their "identity" was not self-generated, genetically received or hoisted on them by their environment. It flowed naturally from their intimacy with God. Their identity was mirrored to them by God. Effortlessly, they radiated the divine "image" and "likeness." They were innocent and free and overflowing with the awareness of God's presence. Adam and Eve experienced themselves as being neither God nor creatures, but the marriage of the two.

As the story goes, a tragedy occurred. Adam and Eve were expelled from the Garden. There was a fall from grace— meaning a fall from God-consciousness into egoic-consciousness. Humanity's "identity" or sense of "self" was no longer tethered to God. In a manner of speaking, conscious contact with God was lost, and we have been

---

[38] Genesis: 3:8

suffering from a case of mistaken identity ever since. It is important to note, however, that our identity in God is not lost, just buried under a veil of illusion.

Given the fact that we are no longer in touch with our God-given identity, we have no choice but to create one—not from truth, but from our feelings, thoughts, judgments, beliefs and misperceptions. And even the best manufactured "self-image" cannot hold a candle to our God-given identity. It is essential to see that our manufactured identities have no foothold in Reality or God. Thus, they are woefully inadequate to handle life's challenges. To the degree that we identify with the manufactured self, we experience painful levels of stress, tension and inadequacy.

Jesus said, "You shall know the truth and the truth shall set you free."[39] An essential aspect of the "truth" that sets us free is our real identity, in God. In other words, the light of God's presence slowly begins to illumine our awareness—revealing to us who we are, in God. I am not talking about an intellectual or conceptual awareness, but an experiential one. Rather than identifying with our habitual self-image or thoughts or emotions, we begin to live from a space of alertness, peace and expansiveness. The soul mirrors God's light. Thus, the fruit of living form our actual identity is strength, compassion, purity, truth, freedom, vitality, wisdom and humility.

---

[39] John 8: 32: often we mistake the True Self" with the personality or the surface self. The personality or surface self is nothing other than a collection of conditioned traits, tendencies, beliefs, assumptions, and emotions—mechanically propelled by life's energies. The "soul" can shine through the personality, but is never reducible to the personality. We are not our bodies, minds and a personalities; each one of us is a soul; and it is the soul that animates the body, mind and spirit. The soul—in its purest form—is the archetype of God.

My first conscious recollection of such an experience—as an adult—occurred a few years into my meditation practice. I was alone in my office, attending to some paper work. Effortlessly, layers of judgment and psychological conditioning simply fell away.[40] There was just open, expansive and liberated awareness—and a sense of presence and fullness and subtle bliss. Life's possibilities seemed endless—not in a manic or grandiose manner, but in a matter of fact kind of way. The only thought that arose was as follows: *"This must be what Adam and Eve experienced on the first day of creation, nothing but freshness and aliveness and freedom."*

Although the experience lingered for a period of time, eventually my conditioned, manufactured and distorted self-returned—along with a familiar level of neurotic judgment and suffering. Yet, I had a taste of something true, good and essential. When I shared this experience with my spiritual director, he said, "You had a contemplative moment, and caught a glimpse of your real self. Your task now is to allow God to grow this Self into your everyday self."

Imagine the very first day of creation: Adam and Eve existed without karma, without conditioning, without compulsion, without fear, without stories, without opinions, without theology, without ideology, without anything impinging on their identity or freedom. Their sense of "self" was mirrored to them not by the parents, but by God. They were free to creatively shape life under the influence of God's love and inspiration, as evidenced by their ability to "name" the

---

40 The only thing that burns in hell is the ego and its many delusions. Hell is not punishment, but purification—the means by which we shed the many layers of the false self.

animals—for to name something is to influence its essence and purpose. Self-realization is a return to Eden, in the sense that we are returning to our true selves: God's image and likeness.[41]

Francis of Assisi would spend whole evenings in prayer, asking "Who are you or Lord, and who am I." The spiritual life is—in part—about the resurrection of God's "image and likeness," as our primary identity. The bottom line is that when we come home to God we do not disappear into a cloud of light, never to be seen again. Rather, we also come home to ourselves—the "Self" that has been hidden in God, since the beginning of time.

Yet, there is an instinctual resistance to shedding the "false self" and living from the "true Self." We are so identified with the false self that we believe we are "it" and "it" is us. So, we want to save "it," perfect "it" and fulfill "it." Letting go of the false self feels like a death of sorts, and it is.

Once after a deep meditative experience, the following words bubbled up into my awareness, *"Craig, do you now understand that self-hatred has nothing to do with God and is a waste of time?"*

Though I experienced this insight as liberating, it also brought a measure of discomfort. It was as if God had

---

[41] God's "image" within us is our capacity for freedom, for love. The more we lovingly exercise our freedom in the service of God and others, the more the "image of God" is resurrected in us. No matter how far we have fallen, our potential for freedom and love remains intact. God's "image" can never be destroyed. God's "likeness" is our capacity to live a God-like life, a life of virtue: joy, love, generosity, wisdom, creativity, nobility, selflessness, etc. Salvation, liberation and or enlightenment is, in part, the restoration of God's "image and likeness" in us.

opened the door of my self-imposed cage, and I was hesitant to fly towards my freedom—because living from soul means letting go of the illusion of control, letting go of the impulse to continually to catch myself, letting go of the stories that have defined me.

Even when we are motivated, however, the false self's grip is a formidable force. The false self can be likened to a gravitational field—the force of which keeps our consciousness mired in the orbit of fear and illusion. Only God's grace is powerful enough to us free from the grip of the false self. Grace is the energy, momentum and might of Divine love and truth operating within creation, for the sole purpose of drawing us home--into God and our identity in God. Simply put, the spiritual life is a process of ever-deepening attunement with those "heavenly powers and principalities" that free us from the tyranny of the false self.

I have learned, however, that the grace of God is most effective in liberating us from the chains of the false self in and through the experience of powerlessness. The false self-thrives on the illusion of control, judgment and cleverness—believing that it has mastery over all of life, even the spiritual life. Powerlessness dissolves our illusionary sense of control, and opens us to what is most authentic and real and actual in us.

An example of this occurred early on in the history of the Assisi Institute. I was trying very, very hard to make everything work—growing the Assisi Institute, nurturing the Assisi Institute, sustaining the Assisi Institute, working the Assisi Institute, etc. In short, I was playing God and guru; and putting unrealistic and enormous levels of pressure on myself—my false self-putting pressure on my false self, to be exact. After leading a day-long retreat, I sat on my apartment steps, exhausted and frustrated. With tears streaming down my face, I prayed, *"Yogananda, I can't keep up with you."*

A small, subtle voice whispered in response, *"I never asked you to keep up with me. Besides, who is in charge of the Assisi Institute?"*

What followed was a sense of deep relief; and a release from the insatiable, unrealistic demands of the false self. A flow of deep, spontaneously prayer flooded my awareness--from my spirit to God's Spirit, marked by an innocent, childlike freedom. I was wonderfully naked to myself and God—not praying to God, but in God. I thought to myself, *"This is how the saints must have prayed."* Intuitively, I knew I was experiencing an aspect of my real Self—a Self -grounded immediately and directly in God's Presence. From that moment forward, I saw that the limitations and inadequacy of the false self was not an occasion for shame, but an opening to grace and my actual identity in God.

What happens, in essence, is that the grace of God elevates us beyond our conditioned thinking, beyond our habitual perceptions and beyond the categories of the mind—enabling us to see as God sees. Such seeing is punctuated by a sense of unity—being able to recognize everyone and everything as existing within the very fabric of the Divine Life. This is precisely how Jesus experienced reality, *"Whatever you do to my brothers and sisters you do unto me."*[42]

There have been a number of practices that have served me well, especially in relationship to the pull of my false self. Sitting in front of an icon of Jesus or Yogananda, breathing consciously, and fixing my attention on their image invariably draws me out of the quagmire of distorted thinking; and into God's loving, expansive consciousness. Prayerfully reading the writings of a saint or a God-illumined sage has often elevated me out of self-delusion. Surrendering my distorted thoughts to God, again and again, tends to clear away any

---

42 Matthew 25:40

perceptual dross. Of course, when I am serving selflessly the needs of others, God's grace moves me above and beyond the tentacles of my personality.

What I am discovering is that the true Self is not a thing or a structure or an object, but a relationship—with God. By contrast, the false self is non-relationship; it is being locked inside of my own painfully distorted thoughts and feeling. At the deepest level of our being, our spirit perpetually touches God's Spirit—or else we would cease to exist. The true Self is the point of contact between our spirit and God's Spirit. We only become conscious of this contact to the degree that we turn our "hearts" and "minds" and "souls" towards God—in an act of love.[43]

God is love. For love to be love it has to be freely given— never forced or compelled. This is why God loves wildly and unconditionally and extravagantly—because God is pure, absolute freedom. Yes, love and freedom are two sides of the same coin. We are made in God's "image." This means that we are capable of loving. And that means that we too are free. No matter how lost we are in delusion or error or sin, the spark of freedom is never extinguished. We are free to love-- to begin the journey back to God.

The moment we turn our hearts towards God in an act of loving freedom, we are beginning to live from our true Selves—because we are breaking out of our isolation and making conscious contact with God. We are moving from the

---

[43] The spirit in us is that part of us that is in perpetual union with God, and is inseparable from God. The spiritual life is, in part, a matter of turning the "eye of the soul" interiorly, towards that point of contact between our spirit and God's Spirit. At this point of contact, it is impossible to discern where God ends and we begin.

surface self to the interior Self—where our spirit touches God's Spirit. Every act of love towards God, every prayer, every meditation, and every sigh directed towards heaven, every heartfelt mantra, and every act of surrender gives God permission to draw us deeper and deeper into His own heart—into conscious union with the Divine Beloved. It is this union that defines us. We become most ourselves—the true Self—when we are married to God, in love and freedom. Our life becomes God's life and God's life becomes our life—union without fusion.

And while our "yes" is always necessary for the journey back to God and the rediscovery of our true Selves, our "yes" is always a response to God's overture—to God's grace. God is the "Good Shepherd" calling out to us, by name. Sometimes "the call" comes in the form of a great joy—like the birth of a child. And sometimes "the call" comes to us under the guise of a loss or some suffering. But it is always a call of love— bidding us to come home. God Always makes the first move. To quote Yoganandaji,

> "O Spirit, I bow to Thee I bow to Thee in front of me, behind me, on the left, and on the right. I bow to Thee above and beneath. I bow to Thee all around me. I bow to Thee within and without. I bow to Thee everywhere, for Thou art everywhere."[44]

To add to the extravagance of it all, it is not just God that responds to us. Heaven too hears us, and comes to our aid. The following quote—from a Sufi tradition—captures beautifully this reality:

> **"The moment a soul turns back towards God so**

---

[44] This prayer poem is taken from Yogananda's "Whispers from Eternity," inspired by the Bhagavad Gita, the Hindu Bible.

much help is given—from the inner plains—where it is invisible. The circumstances in a human being's life begin to rearrange themselves, subtly, from the divine hand. They get everything they need because it is said that the human being going back to God is the pinnacle of creation. Everything in the created world bows down before the human being that dares to turn away from the world to make the journey back to God...that dares to say not my will, but Thy will be done. He (God) is waiting, always watching for those who want to know what it is like to be loved by God."[45]

The rediscovery of our true Selves—in God--is not the end of the story, but the beginning. It reveals our real vocation. To the extent that we live from that point of contact between our spirits and God's Spirit, we become the marriage of heaven and earth. Divinity and creation literally come together, consciously, in us. God and creation are actualized into a loving unity, in us. Through us, God becomes consciously embodied—meaning that God can smile through us, love through us, speak truth through us, heal through us, inspire joy through us, correct through us, create peace through us and inhabit the world through us-consciously and lovingly and purposefully.

Early on in my practice of Kriya Yoga, I was blessed with spontaneous moments of profound bliss, freedom and God-communion. This led me to a distorted expectation relative to the ongoing experience of God's presence. Namely, I came to believe that all that I had to do was passively "let go" and "God's presence" would effortlessly arise within me. Nothing

---

45 Sufism is the mystical branch of Islam, and is marked by an ecstatic love for God. The above quote was given to me during a retreat but the exact source was not cited.

else was needed, ever. I was wrong.

My excessive passiveness eventually resulted in a period of depressive, murky dullness. I mistakenly assumed I was experiencing a "dark night of the soul." Clarity came, however, when I discovered a prayer written by Yogananda, after Francis of Assisi had appeared to him in a vision. The closing lines are as follows,

> *"In waking, eating, working, dreaming, sleeping, serving, meditating, chanting, and divinely loving, my soul constantly hums, unheard by any, God, Christ, Guru."*

After contemplating Yogananda's prayer, I realized that to consistently live from my soul, from the divine image, I had to be vigilant in the exercise of my spiritual will—not in trying to perfect my personality, but in attuning my consciousness to God's consciousness. Simply put, living from my true self is the very act of loving God, turning my attention to God, surrendering my will to God's will. I am only the "me" that God created me to be, fully and entirely, when I am loving—God and others. We become our true selves in the act of loving.

When Jesus spoke to Francis from the San Damiamo Cross, two blessings occurred: Francis heard Jesus "tenderly" speak his name—having the effect of grounding Francis consciously in God. Secondly, Jesus gave Francis a charge, "Go and rebuild my church, can't you see it is crumbling."[46] These two movements are inseparable. We are pulled into a deep and interior union with God, so that we can be God's

---

46 Initially, Francis interpreted Jesus' words literally, and set out rebuilding churches that were in disrepair. He did this with such joy and love, others joined him.

83

living, breathing presence in the world—a holy and beautiful paradox. In living this paradox, we become our true Selves—who God created us to be. Without Francis' union with God, he would have been just a misdirected fanatic. And without Francis' mission, his life would have been little more than an expression of pious solitude. Either way, there would be no "Francis of Assisi" to inspire us, chide us or elevate us. But because Francis said "yes" to both movements of God, he became—in a manner of speaking—another Christ. It is only through loving God and others that we expand into our souls, into our true selves.

All of this became clear one wintery night, about four or five years into my practice of Kriya Yoga. I awoke in the wee hours of the morning. There were two choices before me: to have an unproductive, guilt-inducing orgy with the refrigerator or pray. I decided to pray. My prayer went as follows: *"God, I give my life to you. I want to be at your service. I just want you to do my will."*

Before I share what happened next, let me state in no uncertain terms that I am a very fallible human being, with many faults. I am not the message, just the messenger, and an imperfect one at that. An actual, visible beam of light descended from above, entering me through the top of my head (my crown chakra). As it did, I could actually see the inside of myself—into my soul or spirit. I was awash in light. It was beautiful and blissful, but very intense. It was so intense that I feared it would undo, dissolve or discombobulate me. So, I asked God to please *"Stop the Light"*, and He did.

I believe that my experience of the "light" was an answer to the prayer to be of "service" and to surrender myself to God's "will." Somehow, that light-filled moment paved the way for the Assisi Institute and this book. I have prayed that same prayer many times since—and no downpour of visible light of was forthcoming. Yet, every time we pray to be of service, to be an instrument of love, to do God's will, God floods our spirits with more and more light—until we become light. As the Apostle says, "God is light."[47]

The bottom line is that we become what we love and what we serve. When we love God in the silence of our own interior souls, we become more silent and more peaceful and more still and more steady and more unshakable and more solid and more sacred. And when we lovingly serve God in the world we become larger and wiser and creative and powerful and resourceful and intelligent and loving and compassionate—actually, God becomes these qualities in us and through us, but we do share in God's experience of it all. The following quote from Sri Aurobindo captures dynamics of this process quite succinctly:

> "To walk through life armored against all fear, peril, and disaster, only two things are needed, two that always go together—the grace of the Divine Mother and on your side an inner state made up of faith, sincerity and surrender…. Regard your life as given to you only for the divine work and to help in the divine manifestation…. Let your sincerity and surrender, be genuine and entire. When you give yourself, give completely, without demand, without condition, without reservation so that all in you shall belong to the Divine Mother and nothing shall be left to the ego or given to any other power."[48]

Most of us do not realize the potential that is within us. At the point of contact between our spirits and God's Spirit, all

47 John 1:5

48 "The Dictionary of Sri Aurobindo's Yoga, Compiled by M.P. Pandit, Page 194-195

that is in God is potentially available to us. God is constantly transmitting light from His Spirit to our spirit—and in this light are all the wisdom, strength and grace that we need to fulfill our God-given duties. Too often, though, this light is hidden under our sleepiness, ambivalence, and preoccupations. However, the more willing we are to be an "instrument" of God's love; the more light is given to us.

Life is both complex and challenging. The false self is incapable of skillfully handling the trials that we all face. But when we live from the depths of our souls—in conscious contact with God—all that we need to live wisely and creatively is given to us: strength, wisdom, compassion, patience, clarity, gentleness, endurance, self-control, goodness, peace, love and joy. God's capacities become our capacities—as gift, grace and favor. God's genius becomes our genius.

Think about the many complex functions that occur in the human body, second by second. For example, every three seconds approximately fifty-thousand cells die, and fifty-thousand new cells are produced—each one perfectly capable fulfilling its necessary function in order to sustain life. And all of this occurs without any input or direction from us. It is the intelligence of God—through genetic programming—that orchestrates this complex process.

The wonderful gift of being human is that we have the capability to consciously cooperate with God's purposeful and loving and intelligent designs. Yes, the genius of God is available to us--to guide and direct the course of our lives, to trump karma and direct history. In the prologue to John's Gospel, Jesus is described as being God's "Word" "In the beginning was the Word and the Word was with God and the Word was God.... And the Word became flesh and dwelt among us."[49] The "Word of God" is the "mind" or "logos" or "intelligence" of God. Jesus was the very incarnation of God's organizing brilliance. And by God's grace—along with our silence, humility and faith—our consciousness can become an instrument of God's highest, most loving designs. Typically, this capacity to align our awareness with the mind of God is referred to as "intuition." Intuition allows us to experience the direct perception of truth without the intermediary of the senses.

The quote below, will help to clarify this notion of intuition:

> "Intuition is the cooperation of human intelligence with superhuman wisdom. It creates the link between the absolute and the relative, between the supernatural and the natural, between faith and reason."[50]

In Adam and Eve's fall from grace, humankind's capacity for intuition became obscured under the dross of ignorance, arrogance and emotional confusion—but never destroyed. In a manner of speaking, the spiritual life is a return to the "Garden of Eden." "Eden" is not, however, the absence of pain or challenges. It is certainly not a utopian existence. It is intimacy with God. It is walking hand and hand with God— sometimes in light and sometimes in darkness. It is the restoration of the image of God in us—not in a future heaven, but here and now. In the discovery of our identity in God—what Yogananda referred to as Self-realization—we rediscover our capacity to hear God's voice; it comes in the form of conscience, inspiration and intuition.

Practically speaking, beginning each day with meditation creates within me a zone of silence. From this place of

---

49 John 1:3 and 14

50 *Meditations* on the Tarot," Valentin Tomberg, page 536

silence, there is often an intuitive knowing or wisdom that guides my choices—not just in spiritual matters, but in practical decisions too. When I am unclear as to the best course of action in a particular situation, I bring my awareness back to the interior zone of silence, and ask God for guidance or clarity or direction. Sooner or later, unfailingly, an answer arrives—either from within me or from a friend or from some other source. Often, I simply pray to be an instrument of God's love; God loves to answer this kind of prayer, immediately. The bottom line is that when I live from my true self, my soul, our lives become a perpetual partnership--with God.

We all want to live a good life, a creative life, and a blessed life. We are genetically programmed for maximum joy, peace, and unity—within and without. These "values" and "virtues" are attainable, not by one's own cleverness, but by the grace and energy of God. Though the grace of God comes to us in many forms, we must eventually make room for it in ourselves, in the very depths of being, where our spirit touches God's Spirit—where streams of living water flow perpetually. We must learn to drink from these streams of living waters and to be sustained by theme--moment by moment.

Please don't misunderstand me. As we gravitate towards God, we must also become intimately aware of all the psychological, emotional and behavioral possibilities that reside within our psyches. Everything must be brought into the light of consciousness—our consciousness and God's Consciousness. For me, this means being ruthlessly honest with myself—not to fix my personality, but to surrender all of my energy and potential and humanity to God; so that God is free to divinize every aspect of my life.

I am no longer trying to find myself in myself. Rather, I am discovering myself in God, and discovering God in my-Self.

The grand paradox is that as I discover my identity in God, I am able to be more present, more compassionate, and more loving towards others; and my service to the world becomes clearer and more fruitful.

Saint Bonaventure wrote of Saint Francis and his absolute willingness to be an instrument of God's will:

> "Francis had reached such purity,
> That his body was in remarkable harmony
> With his spirit,
> And his spirit with God.
> As a result a result God ordained
> That creation which serves its Maker
> Should be subject in an extra-ordinary way
> to his Francis' will and command."[51]

---

[51] "The Life of Saint Francis, " Saint Bonaventure Page 52

6 CHRIST CONSCIOUSNESS: GOD AS RELATIONSHIP

If anyone says, "I love God," and hates his brother is a liar; for he who has does not love his brother whom he has seen, cannot love God whom he has not seen. -The Apostle John

Love is God, not merely as the noblest sentiment of a poet, but as an aphorism of eternal truth. - Sri Yukteswar

God is Love. - Yogananda and the Apostle John

It was halftime at my son's basketball game, and I was sitting alone in the bleachers watching the other parents, kids, players and coaches all around me. Spontaneously, their expressions, sounds, movements, colors, shapes and sizes started melding into something exquisite, touching my heart in a way I had never experienced before.

"Everyone is so beautiful, loveable, and filled with light," I thought. *"I wish they could see themselves I wish they could see themselves as I am seeing them now. This must be how God sees us."*

Then my heart, already wide open, expanded into a sea of what could only be pure love--a unified field of loving consciousness, without emotion or sentimentality. My sense of self swelled far beyond my body and mind. There was only that one, indivisible love, and we were all part and parcel of it. For a brief instant, I was no longer the "me" that I had been. I was an aspect of the love that undergirds everything and everyone. I had no individual thoughts, opinions, or conceptualizations, just the all-encompassing unity that is Love – or God.

"What if I don't get out of this expanded state?"

The fears started creeping in: *"What if the 'I' that I know to be 'me' does not return? How can I function or make a living?"* Almost immediately, I was right back where I started--sitting alone in the bleachers on a wintery day, waiting for the second half of the game to begin.

Yet, somehow, my experience of myself and others was forever altered. Since that moment, I have a greater capacity for empathy, a moral impulse toward inclusivity, and a heightened sense of kinship with everyone. I am less consumed with my own suffering and more attuned to the pain of others. I was given, in all humility, a glimpse of reality as seen through the eyes of God.

While we experience separateness, God experiences unity. Though imbued with individuality, our lives arise from a common Source, and are sustained by that Source. The life force that nourishes my life is the same life force that nourishes all of life—radiating from God's Spirit. The intelligence regulating the many complex functions within my body is the very same intelligence that orders creation. Whether we are Jew or Gentile, black or white, liberal or conservative, we are brothers and sisters in God.

"While we recognize the relative existence of differences, yet we must not only know intellectually, but realize spiritually, that One Life pervades everything," wrote Yogananda.[52]

It's not enough to experience Self-realization, or our real identity in God. For our relationship with God to fully ripen, we must be willing to have our hearts and minds opened to experience of God's presence within all of creation. As a child, I was rightly taught to bow before the presence of Christ in the Blessed Sacrament.[53] Given the fact God dwells in all of us, should we not also bow before one another?

"This is our whole metaphysics: emanation, exemplarity, consummation; to be illumined by spiritual rays and to be led back to the highest Reality...Just as you see that a ray of light entering through a stained glass window is colored in different ways according to the different colors of the various parts, so the divine ray shines forth in different ways and in different properties...Creatures are shadows, echoes and pictures of that first, most powerful, most wise and most perfect Principal...They are vestiges, representations, spectacles proposed to us and signs divinely given so that we can see God."[54]

The peace and stillness of contemplation is not the final frontier, but a starting point. God also calls us outside of ourselves, to touch and know the Divine presence in every part and particle of creation. This includes earth and sky, plants and animals, friends and enemies, believers and

---

[52] Paramahansa Yogananda, "Journey to Self-Realization," 347-348

[53] The term "Blessed Sacrament" refers to the consecrated bread and wine Catholics and Orthodox Christians hold to be the "Body" and "Blood" of Jesus

[54] Hecaem, 17 (V, 332 and XXI, 14, V, 386)

nonbelievers. While we see competing tribes, warring clans, beloved insiders and cursed outsiders, God sees us as one family, united in the Divine Presence.

The goal of mature spirituality is to expand our capacity for experience, so that we can experience creation as God does: as one seamless garment. This is not a luxury, but a requirement. According to Saint Bonaventure, "The universe is a ladder by which we ascend to God."[55] Saint Paul tells us the ultimate goal of spiritual life is the experience of "God being all in all."[56] Yogananda refers to the direct experience of God in creation as "Christ-Consciousness: The projected consciousness of God immanent in all of creation...Great saints and yogis know this as the state of Samadhi meditation wherein their consciousness has become identified with the divine intelligence in every particle of creation; they feel the entire universe in their own body."[57]

At a certain point in my practice of Kriya Yoga, I began to experience a tension of sorts. My youngest son was off to college, my psychotherapy practice was functioning smoothly, and I was very content living a celibate life. I was relatively comfortable, peaceful, and settled. I even had thoughts of pursuing a monastic lifestyle. So the tension started bubbling up when I felt a different calling, and I met Vicki Jo.
We met by accident, God's "accident" to be exact. I was looking for new office space, so I called a colleague who had an office to rent. She showed me the space. I liked what I saw, and wrote a check for the first month's rent.

"My business partner is out of town, donating one of her

---

[55] Saint Bonaventure, "The soul's Journey Into God," page 2
[56] 1 Corinthians: 15:28
[57] Paramahansa Yogananda: "The Second Coming of Christ," Vol. II, page 1581

kidneys to her younger sister," my colleague stated. "I am sure she won't mind that I've rented the space to you."

When Vicki Jo returned, she did mind.

"I just want you to know I don't need any more friends," she bluntly stated when we met.

"What makes you think I want to be your friend?" I responded.

Sometimes God writes straight with crooked lines, meaning long before romance was on the horizon, we actually became very good friends. Our friendship was based on a spiritual foundation. Vicki Jo had been raised in a wonderful Italian Catholic family. She was naturally a person of deep prayer, strength and compassion. Though we had much in common by way of culture, interests and education, it was our spiritual connection that grounded our relationship. Long before there was a first kiss, we had become best friends who supported, accepted and encouraged each other. Much to our mutual surprise, we were learning to take care of each other's souls.

As our relationship evolved, a part of me wanted to remain in my spiritual cocoon. I had a clear sense of the worth of prolonged, sustained solitude. Yet, I also knew the value of a lovingly active life, and I felt drawn to marriage and a calling to serve others by teaching Kriya yoga. To put it mildly, I was ambivalent. My ambivalence began to clear on two levels. The first came in a flash of clarifying insight or wisdom while reading a book written by a trusted mentor.

> My life is not about me...
> This is what saints know and we don't
> This is why we don't really understand saints.
> This is why masters cannot teach many people.

This is why there are many masters.
Most people think their lives are about them.
And they aren't.[58]

In short, I began realizing my life was about something far greater than my own wishes and preferences. Real happiness, I came to realize, comes from allowing our little lives to be used by a greater life--God's life. To paraphrase the words of Mary, the Blessed Mother, it is allowing "our lives to be done unto us, by God."

On another level, my conflicting feelings began to settle as the result of a persistent intuition. Authentic intuition is actually the development of conscience. Often, we focus on the negative aspect of conscience, experienced as a pang of discomfort, disapproval, or warning. The positive side of conscience is an impulse of recommendation or guidance, experienced as peace, joy or expansive clarity. In the words of Christian mystic Valentin Tomberg, "Conscience is the door, the sole legitimate one, to a world at least as vast, and much more profound, than the world we perceive with the senses."[59] Simply put, I found myself increasingly drawn, with wonder and awe, to both the married life and a life of service.

Whether we are talking about a romantic relationship, a friendship, or a sense of community, the true basis for unity and harmony is not "good will" alone, but the radiation of Christ Consciousness: God's guiding, organizing and designing intelligence operating within creation—working to unify the human family. On the night before he died, Jesus said to his disciples, "I no longer call you servants, for the servant does not know what his master is doing; but I have

---

[58] Richard Rohr, Adam's return," The Crossroad Publishing Company, Page 66.
[59] Valentin Tomberg, "Meditations on the Tarot," Page 511.

called you friends, for all that I have heard from my Father I have made known to you."[60]

No matter how well intentioned we might be, the gravitational pull of the ego and unconscious forces are too great for us to overcome by our own strength. True unity or friendship is the fruit of God's Spirit, inspiring us, empowering us, and elevating us beyond our natural abilities and instincts. Despite our best efforts, we cannot liberate ourselves, because we are part of the problem. Something greater is needed: God's elevating, all-powerful love.

> "It was the consummate, unselfish love which Jesus bestowed on his disciples by addressing them as friends, souls whom he highly esteemed...Such friendship is truly of God, for purely selfless sacrifice is possible only when human love partakes of God's love. When one can express the almighty power of intoxicating divine love, it awakens the living heart of God's love in the lives of others."[61]

A key moment in the evolution of our relationship came when I realized we were becoming a romantic couple. I was scared, not of commitment, but of making a mistake by misinterpreting God's will for our relationship. So I literally got on my knees and prayed.

> *"Jesus and Yogananda, I don't want to hurt Vicki Jo or myself. If it is not God's will we come together as a couple, please make it known. Not my will, but God's will be done.."*

Intuitively, the answer seemed to simply descend from above:

---

[60] John 15:15

[61] ParamahansaYogananda, "The Second Coming," Page 1400

"You have been brought together not only for your own love, but to be of loving service to others."

In Genesis, God tells Adam and Eve "be fruitful and multiply."[62]   Yes, the joy of romantic love is to be appreciated, enjoyed and celebrated. Yet it is also meant to be generative – shared, given away, fruitful. Marriage works best when it is serving something greater than a couple's happiness, most often in the form of children, societal needs and spiritual causes. By lovingly serving others, couples paradoxically deepen their own experience of love – because God is love.

After much prayer, discernment and feedback from spiritual mentors, Vicki Jo and I made a trip to Assisi, Italy. Joined by a few family members and friends, we exchanged vows while standing in the shadow of Francis and Clare. We were blessed to have our vows witnessed by a very holy monk who loves Jesus, Francis and Yogananda.

"You are husband and wife, forever and forever," he stated very strongly at the conclusion of the wedding ceremony.

Vicki Jo is not only my wife, but my very best friend. Whatever wounds linger from my childhood, God is healing through her sweet and steady love. I have learned to depend on her wisdom, welcome her gentle correction, and cherish her affection. In the highest heaven there are no husbands and wives per se. However, I know our love will endure throughout eternity--because our love is a participation in God's unending love.

Without her strength, hard work and prayerful insight, I

---

[62] Genesis 1:28

could not lead the Assisi Institute. We are not two pillars helping to hold up the Assisi Institute, we are one pillar serving God, Christ and Yogananda. Coincidentally, Vicki Jo's confirmation name is Clare. Mine is Francis. We are deeply devoted to both Saints, and see their selfless love as a model for our own.

The ultimate basis for a happy and fruitful life together is not sexual chemistry or the ability to communicate on an intimate level – though these are important. No, it is friendship rooted in God. In the words of Yogananda, "Two persons who unite their lives to help each other toward divine realization are found their marriage on the right basis: unconditional friendship."[63]

While on our earthly sojourn, friendship is the greatest gift we can possibly enjoy--provided it is rooted in Christ Consciousness. True spiritual friendship draws us out of isolation, out of the partitions of ego-consciousness, and out of self-absorption. God's light shining uniquely in and through us recognizes the light shining in and through others. Thus, the bond of true friendship is at the level of the soul. Soul-friendship recognizes the "luminous seed of God" in each other, and seeks to serve its full flowering.

> "Friendship is the purest form of God's love because it is born of the Heart's free choice and is not imposed upon us by familial instinct. Ideal friends never part; nothing can sever their fraternal friendship...All true friends you have made you will meet again in the home of the Father, for real love is never lost."[64]

---

[63] This quote was given to me on a retreat I attended, and attributed to Yogananda.

[64] Paramahansa Yogananda: "Where There Is Light," Self-Realization Fellowship, page 142

I am blessed with a number of deep, soulful friendships in addition to my wife. My oldest friend is Mike. Our Italian mothers walked us in strollers together, but we didn't actually have our first play date until we were six. We fought. The next time we got together, he stole my rifle. Despite the rough start, our friendship flourished. He was the pitcher and I the catcher on our Little League team. I fixed him up with Carol, who became his wife and bore him six children (I don't know if Carol has ever forgiven me for that!) We are godfathers to each other's firstborn.

While our friendship has deep human roots, it is ultimately grounded in God. As young adolescents, we often trudged off to church on Saturday afternoons to attend confession. On the way home, we would declare our desire to be really holy – which mean we would do our best not to have "dirty thoughts." At sixteen, we both underwent deep conversion experiences. To this day, we buoy each other with laughter, words of spiritual encouragement, and reminders of God's faithfulness. Most importantly, we touch and inspire one another at a deep, soulful level. Our friendship is food for my soul.

God surprised me with another true friend during a Kriya Yoga conference in the summer of 2007. Swami Nirvananada led us in devotional chanting during a morning meditation service. As Swamiji (my affectionate nickname for him) sang, the presence of God resonated in his voice and music. I was drawn out of myself into a heavenly space. I knew he loved God, deeply. I was determined to speak with him.

When we first sat together, I experienced a jolt of profound recognition. Looking into each other's eyes, our souls touched. Nothing needed to be acknowledged or stated. We were spiritual brothers, pure and simple – and will be for all eternity. I was thrilled to discover he was deeply devoted to Jesus, Francis and Yogananda. He effortlessly bubbled with spiritual joy, in a Franciscan way. I believe our meeting was the reunion of old friends, rooted in God.

Swamiji was born Giorgio Kiegsch in Trieste, Italy. After reading An Autobiography of a Yogi in 1975, he began his spiritual search in earnest. He was initiated into Kriya yoga, and then made a pilgrimage to India. There, he volunteered with Mother Teresa's Sisters of Charity, helping care for the destitute of Calcutta. Eventually, Swamiji met Father Marian Zelazek, who was helping the children of lepers in Puri, a city in eastern India. He asked how he could help Father Zelazek, who responded by giving him photographs of seven children who lived in the leper colony. He asked Swamiji to seek sponsors for them.

Swamiji began performing kirtans (a form of devotional chanting) throughout Italy to raise money for the Puri children. Now he performs hundreds of kirtans every year in the United States, Europe and India in support of Father Zelazek's work. The funds have helped build schools, hostels, and a center that provides housing and job training for young girls caught in the horrors of organized prostitution. They have also helped disabled girls learn trades and put food in the mouths of children who would otherwise go hungry. Though celibate, Swamiji has many, many spiritual children. In short, I have come to believe he is a living saint, combining his deep love for God with service to the poor.

Once a year, Swamiji visits the Assisi Institute, blessing us with his music, infectious bliss and generous spirit. When we take people on pilgrimage to Assisi, Italy, he often joins us and deepens the experience for all. Daily, I thank God for Swamiji's presence in my life. He is overflowing with Christ Consciousness. Not only is he a friend, he is a spiritual brother and confidant. I have given him permission to correct me, whenever he thinks it's needed. I trust him that much.[65]

An important aspect of Christ Consciousness -- God's love and intelligence permeating creation -- is the presence of a spiritual father or mother. I am blessed to have such a figure in my life, Father Richard Rohr. I first spotted him in a film I viewed while in college. As I watched him deliver a sermon, I was captivated. It was not because he was a great orator, but because of the truth that emanated in and through his words. They touched my spirit in a deep and profound manner. At that time, Richard had not yet written any books. He had published a number of talks and retreats on cassette tapes, which I eagerly listened to--spiritual food for my soul.

I was almost 30 when I finally met him. I was the religious education director at an active church in my diocese and had made arrangements for Richard to give the parish a weeklong retreat. I remember picking him up at the airport as if it happened yesterday. I nervously awaited his arrival, wondering if he would like me – or if I would like him in person. I was not disappointed. His warmth, love, selflessness and wisdom were immediately apparent, and my consciousness was easily elevated to a peaceful, sublime state.

At one point during his stay, I walked into a darkened room and found Richard sitting cross legged on the floor, silently praying the rosary in front of a lit candle. I quietly sat next to him and felt a blanket of peaceful silence envelop me. I was simply in God, without a thought or care or concern. I did not want the moment to end. It did, of course, but the powerful sense of God's peace lingered for weeks.

---

[65] The ego is far too capable of self-delusion. Thus, we need to be open to feedback from mature and trusted individuals.

At the end of his stay, I asked if I could be one of his spiritual sons. Without hesitation, Richard hugged me and said, "Of course." To be a son or daughter to a spiritual father or mother implies a willingness to sit at their feet, learn from them, seek their counsel, attune your awareness to their consciousness, and to be open to correction whenever it is needed. Such a relationship is not based on control or subservience, but on mutual love and respect. Richard has never wanted me to be dependent on him, never ordered me to obey him, and encouraged me to think for myself. He simply wants me to be happy and healthy as I surrender myself to God.

One of the greatest gifts Richard has given me is the ability to trust my own internal sense of God's will for my life. Early in our relationship, I had to make a tough decision that I knew would draw severe criticism from some. Not knowing what to do, I called him.

> "Richard, I trust you completely and whatever guidance you give, I will take as God's will for my life."

> "I love you," he said, after a pausing for a moment. "I wish I could be there with you. I don't know what you should do. But if you trust me, then trust yourself, because I trust you. And I trust that whatever you prayerfully decide will be what God wills for you. I don't say this to everyone, but I do say it to you. Trust yourself, because I trust you!"

His influence has been powerful and formative in my life. Once, he sent me a letter and at the conclusion, he wrote: "Because of your childhood trauma, you will probably experience some level of wounded-ness for the rest of your life. Craig, always carry your wounds gracefully. Remember, our wounds are the portals by which God's grace enters our lives. So carry them gracefully!"

He was correct. Some of my childhood wounds have lingered, and bring a degree of pain and discomfort. Often, I remember Richard's words and endeavor to prayerfully carry my wounds with grace.

On another occasion, we were driving in my car and he made an unexpected pronouncement.

"It's a good thing that you had the childhood you had," he told me, out of the blue.

"How can you say that?" I was incredulous. "I am spending thousands of dollars in therapy every year trying to heal my inner child, fix myself and find happiness."

"I know you had a tough childhood, but you are gifted. If you were not wounded, you'd probably just be another yuppie making lots of money and contributing nothing of real value to the world. Instead, you've become a healer of the wounded, and you are making a real difference in the world. Perhaps your childhood is not a mistake. Perhaps it was the childhood God intended you to have."

I stopped dead in my tracks. If the childhood I had was the one I was meant to have, then I was not a victim. God's grace was at work through it all. Instead of trying to fix everything from the past, I could ask God what he wanted me to do with it. That was the beginning of a personal revolution in my life. In all situations, I stopped being a victim and started trusting in God's providence.

Nearly 30 years has gone by since Richard came into my life. Do we always agree on the nuances of theological and philosophical articulation? No. Our love is much deeper. I thank God for Richard's friendship daily. I feel a loving gratitude for him that is too great to express with words. Just a few years ago, while visiting the Assisi Institute, Richard complimented my work and then asked if he still had permission to correct me when needed.

"Yes, of course," I answered.

Lastly, I'd like to reflect on my relationship with my biological father. As I mentioned earlier, he was a severe alcoholic. While living with my foster parents, I continued to have a relationship with him. It was an emotionally distant one, however, until my freshman year in college. I received a phone call from the woman he was dating.

"Your father is at the doctor's office, he suffered an apparent stroke."

I immediately set out to his home, via a Greyhound Bus. When I arrived, I was sure he had suffered a stroke. The right side of his face was drooping, along with the whole left side of his body.

He immediately assured me, "I have not suffered a stroke. The doctor told me I have polyneuritis, an inflammation of the nerves."

"What does that mean? What caused it? What is the prognosis?"

"It is caused from alcohol abuse," he explained. "The doctor said that if I stop drinking, it will clear up in a matter of weeks. If I don't stop drinking, he said I will be dead in a month or two."

After a very pregnant pause, I answered, "Well?"

"Well, I am going to stop drinking, immediately. I need

your prayers. Will you pray for me?"

"Yes Dad. I will pray for you, every day. I love you."

"Thanks. I love you too."

My father lived for another seventeen years; and he never drank again. He returned to church, made amends to everyone he had hurt, was a wonderful grandfather and died with a measure of interior peace. He even attended a two-hour therapy session with me. I wish that session was taped. We both spoke from the depths of our hearts. I don't think I ever felt closer to him than I did during that session.

During his final years, our relationship was not perfect, but it was good and loving and supportive. I continue to pray for him every day--intuitively knowing that my prayers reach him as waves of light and joy. The love we have for each other is stronger than death, because it is an expression of the one love—God's love. I am absolutely sure that we shall see each other again and our love will be perfected, in God.

The relationships we have do not dissolve into nothingness at death, nor are they lost in some impersonal light. They are, for sure, resurrected into new life—into the Divine Life. Creation is not an accidental event and history is not an incidental occurrence; they are the means whereby God expresses His love, His intelligence and His providence. Everything matters to God, most especially our relationships, because everything is pierced with His love and wisdom.[66]

I will close with a story from my Catholic School Days. I was

---

[66] The incarnation of God, in Jesus, proclaims a universal truth: namely, God has entered fully into the human condition, not just generally, but personally—as a force of love and spiritual evolution..

in sixth grade. It was a Friday afternoon and we were given the rare treat of viewing a movie. As we were being silently herded into an empty classroom, I made the mistake of speaking to a classmate. My indiscretion brought a swift question from Sister Minelpha, "Mr. Bullock would like to have us listen to him rather than watch the movie. Should we accommodate him?" In a unified chorus of voices my classmates responded, along with a chorus of dirty looks, "No Sister."

"Should I send Mr. Bullock back to the classroom, to do work, by himself?"

Gleefully they answered, "Yes Sister."

To which she replied, "I'd like to, but I think Mr. Bullock needs to watch this movie, so that he can figure out what is really important in life. Are you willing to keep your big mouth closed Mr. Bullock?"

"Yes Sister."

"Then you can stay for the movie," she stated, as she winked lovingly in my direction.

The move was about Father Damien, a missionary priest from Belgium.[67] The essence of the story is that he spent sixteen years caring for the physical, spiritual and emotional needs of an entire leper colony; eventually contracting leprosy himself. Despite his disease, he continued to vigorously and lovingly serve his fellow lepers and planned for the continuation of the programs he developed after his death. He died, amidst his community of lepers, in 1889, at the age

---

[67] Father Damien was canonized a saint by Pope Benedict on December 11, 2009

of 49.

As soon as the movie ended, my hand shot up and a question followed leaped out of my mouth, "Sister, did he know he might get leprosy before going to the colony?"

"Yes. Of course he did."

"Then why did he go?

"The love of Christ within him compelled him to love and serve the lepers, who also had Christ inside of them."

"But he died of leprosy." I protested.

"Some things are more important than self-preservation, like those who need our love. A good life is not determined by personal pleasure, but the willingness to go beyond self-preoccupation and to serve others."

To this very day, I still marvel at the imprint that the Father Damien story left on my young, tender psyche. Even during the most self-indulgent phase of my life, I would think of that movie and Sister Minelpha's wise words. They haunted me, rightly so, as an authentic pang of conscience. The Father Damien story continues to be an archetypal point on my moral and spiritual compass, calling me to deeper and deeper levels of surrender—to the wisdom, love and presence of the Christ Consciousness permeating everyone and everything.

It is important to note that Father Damien was not merely a humanitarian—meaning that it was not self-generated altruism that motivated him. True spirituality is something far beyond any form of self-mastery. Father Damien was inspired by a "Power" greater than himself. The very same "Energy" and "Wisdom" that was at work in Jesus of Nazareth was at work within Father Damien—that is, God's Love and

Wisdom. The "Good News" is that the Love and Wisdom of God are also at work within us—drawing us away from ignorance, out of isolation, and into the experience of ecstatic union with God, in and through creation.

Francis' canticle, "Brother Sun and Sister Moon" perfectly captures the essence of Christ Consciousness:

"Most High, all-powerful, all-good Lord, All praise is Yours, all glory, all honor, and all blessings. To you alone, Most High, do they belong, and no mortal is worthy to pronounce Your Name. Praised be you my Lord with all your creatures, especially Sir Brother Sun, Who is the day through whom you give us light. And he is beautiful and radiant with great splendor, of You most High, he bears the likeness. Praised be You, my Lord, through Sister Moon and the stars, in the heavens you have made them bright, precious and fair.

Praised be You, my Lord, through Brothers Wind and Air, and fair and stormy, all weather's moods, by which you cherish all that you have made.

Praised be you my Lord through Sister Water, so useful, humble, precious and pure.

Praised be You my Lord through our Sister, Mother Earth who sustains and governs us, producing varied fruits with colored flowers and herbs. Praised be You my Lord through those who grant you pardon for love of You and bear sickness and trial.

Blessed are those who endure in peace, by You Most High they will be crowned.

Praised be You, my Lord through Sister Death, from whom no-one living can escape. Woe to those who die in mortal sin. Blessed are they She finds doing Your will. No second death can do them harm.

Praise and bless my Lord and give Him thanks, and serve Him with great humility."

7 THE MARRIAGE OF THE SOUL TO GOD

I am the vine, you are the branches. He that abides in me and I in him, brings forth much fruit." - Jesus

Those who venerate Me, giving over all activities to Me, contemplating Me by single- minded yoga—remaining absorbed in Me—indeed, O Arjuna, for those whose consciousness is fixed in Me, I become their redeemer..." - Bhagavad Gita

A key moment in my spiritual evolution came during a conversation with a wise, old monk.

"Craig, you can see all the therapists in the world, but it won't make a difference," he told me. "You are only going to be at peace with yourself when you surrender to God, entirely." Intuitively, his words rang true. Surrender is an ever-deepening process, but it begins with a loving, decisive choice to make God the centerpiece of our lives, indeed the love of our lives.

In her book, *Interior Castles,* Teresa of Avila clearly and poetically describes the various stages of the spiritual life. It is a love affair whereby we "betroth" ourselves to God. At the auspicious moment, when God wills it, a consummation occurs: the union or "marriage" of our souls to God.

"When the soul approaches the Beloved now, He bestows upon her the kiss sought by the bride. And enfolded in this kiss are all the other blessings that come with every degree of prayer that has unfolded along the soul's journey home to Him. It is my understanding, that here in this dwelling that all the soul has been longing for is fulfilled. Here the wounded soul is given abundant water to drink. Here the soul delights beneath God's holy tent."[68]

My own betrothal to God began to morph towards a marriage a few years after I started initiating people into Kriya Yoga. Though growing, the Assisi Institute was still a "mom and pop" operation with one part-time staff member, a rented space for meditation, and a very meager budget. Then, I received a phone message from an old business associate.

"Craig, I have a building to sell you. It's 22,000 square feet and comes with a chapel, retreat rooms, offices, and a couple of acres of land. I'll hold the mortgage, no money down. Call me!"

Immediately, I called a Board of Directors meeting. We hastily put together a fund drive, created a business plan and prayerfully attempted to discern God's will. We decided to buy the building. As a spiritual community, we knew we were being asked to move beyond a comfortable, cozy existence. God was asking a great deal of us, calling on us to be a force-

---

68 "The Interior Castle," Teresa of Avila, transalated by Mirabai Starr, Page 283

field of truth, beauty and goodness. The challenge was as daunting as it was inspiring.

One evening during dinner, I turned to Vicki Jo, my new bride, "If we buy this building, it is going to demand a colossal commitment on my part, for the rest of my life. I will have to give all of myself to God. I can't hold any part of myself back, at all. God has to have every bit of my energy, imagination and will," I told her.

"I know," she responded, without batting an eye.

"You didn't sign up for this when you married me. I don't feel as if I'm being fair to you, yet I can't do it without you. If it is going to happen," I told her, "I need you by my side. We have to be in this together. But if you cannot commit to this adventure, I'll entirely understand. I will interpret your 'no' as a sign from God that this enterprise is not meant to be. Either way, I will be at peace. In fact, I will even be a bit relieved if you say you can't do it."

Vicki took my hand.

"Does the thought of it overwhelm me? Yes, of course. But I love the ride God and you are taking me on. Why do you think I married you? We've got to play this hand out. Don't you dare take the easy way out of this opportunity, understand? Give God all you've got."

She leaned in and gently kissed me on the mouth.

"Let's do it," she said
.

Teary-eyed, I replied, "Okay."

At that moment, I realized God was lovingly demanding every fiber of my being. Please don't misunderstand me: any success experienced by the Assisi Institute is the fruit of God's grace and Yogananda's guidance. Yet, human will is also needed. While God's will effortlessly unfurls in heaven, here on earth our "yes" is essential to its unfolding.

"Know the work of redemption, being that of love, requires the perfect union of two wills, distinct and free – divine will and human will...Thus miracles require two united wills! They are not manifestations of an all-powerful ordaining, but are due to a new power which is born whenever there is a unity between divine will and human will."[69]

To the extent our will is aligned with the Divine will, we become a point of contact and concentration for God's highest, most evolutionary purposes here on earth. With the new building, it was clear God wanted more from me, my wife and all of us: a deep, collective "yes" to God's work of liberation, which is simply the willingness to embody God's love and light for a confused and frightened world.

When we sincerely betroth ourselves to God, we give God permission to place us in situations that challenge us to the core. This is not to punish us, but to awaken the deepest layers of our souls. We learn to say "yes" to God from levels of our spirit we did not know existed. Through it all, God is rousing us from our slumber, resurrecting our capacities for wisdom, generosity, creativity, and joy--fashioning us into instruments of His love.

Through prayerful discernment, Vicki Jo and I determined that we needed to somehow deepen our commitment to God, Jesus and Yogananda—so as to expand our capacity to be instruments of God's will. What came to us, interestingly enough, were the three vows associated with Catholic

---

[69] "Meditations on the Tarot," Valentin Tomberg, pages 56-57.

Religious Orders: poverty, chastity and obedience. Upon reading some of the Yogic Scriptures, such as the Bhagavad Gita, I discovered that these vows are not unique to Catholicism. They are present, in some form or another, in all mystical traditions. They are the ultimate expression of the aspiration to surrender everything to God.

In September of 2011 Vicki Jo, a core group of our Assisi family and myself stood before the aforementioned Swami Nirvanananda, and took the vows of poverty, obedience and chastity. We did this not only for our own spiritual edification, but in service to the work of Christ, Yogananda and the lineage of the Kriya Gurus.[70]

Let me explain how the vows work. The vow of poverty, especially as it pertains to householders, is not primarily associated with the giving up of money or material possessions—though it does imply a simple life-style. More poignantly, it is a letting go of what we think we know and the willingness to release our agendas. In other words, poverty is standing naked and unprotected before God—thus giving God permission to take possession of us. It is finding our security in God alone. Poverty is allowing God to empty us of our personal desires, emotions, and imagination. The essence of the vow of poverty can be easily gleaned from a story in the life of Francis.

Apparently, Francis was causing too much of a stir among the people of his town. In response, the local bishop closed down Francis' growing community. Francis decided to go to Rome and ask the Pope if he was doing something wrong.

---

[70]At the Assisi Institute, we refer to these vows as the "path of discipleship." The process can be likened to the secular "Third Orders" within the Catholic Church.

He wasn't going to Rome to plead his case or assert his rights. He wanted the truth, no matter what it might cost him. He was humble, childlike and teachable. Francis had a beginner's mind. Thus, he was capable of receiving wisdom from men and God.

A superficial understanding of the vow of poverty might interpret it as a form of masochism. Nothing, however, could be further from the truth. Interior poverty prepares the soul to receive, from the hand of God, that which is new and unexpected and marvelous and unspeakable and necessary. Simply put, Spiritual poverty gives God permission to be wildly generous towards us!

Living the vow of poverty is always a process. We must be patient and compassionate with ourselves—because God is patient and compassionate with us. We must never think, however, that we have plumed the depths of poverty. There are always more attachments to surrender, and more truth and beauty and goodness to receive—from God.

Following the vow of poverty is the vow of obedience, which must be placed in its proper context. In reading Yogananda's writings, I am always struck by the fact that he simply believed God becomes personal and knowable—in varying degrees--through saints, sages and avatars. For example, Yogananda accepted the truth that Jesus was conceived under the power of the Holy Spirit, was born of the Virgin Mary and is the very incarnation of God's "Wisdom" or "Intelligence" or "Mind." This means, for example, that Jesus' words arise from the Great Silence, and are wholly pure, reliable and trustworthy—capable of washing away all manner of delusion and ushering us into the very Consciousness of God.

The vow of obedience, therefore, is the opposite of tyranny or slavery or oppression. It is the sustained willingness to be in alignment with truth--God's truth; the fruit of such alignment to is liberation from suffering. What I have come to discover is that God's truth is not primarily a theological construct but an organizing power that sets things right, arranges circumstances to serve our highest evolution, and propels us towards deeper levels of enlightenment.

Obedience is realizing that there is a reality "higher" than oneself. Obedience is recognizing God, and yielding to God's Truth and Beauty and Goodness. The fruit of obedience is, therefore, enhanced common sense, mental clarity, balance, poise, strength, endurance, discernment, inspired intuition, peace, joy and a greater capacity for love.

I must admit, obedience does not come easily for me. It requires a deep level of trust, trust of spiritual authority to be exact. Reaching far back into my childhood, I always wanted to call my own shots; that tendency has not disappeared, Yet, I have come to realize that the only thing that makes sense in this world is God's will—because God's will is the fullness of Truth, Beauty and Goodness.

Whatever historical blights Christianity has brought upon itself through the ages, it cannot be denied that the Consciousness of Christ has produced great saints—such as Gregory of Nyssa, Augustine, Francis, Clare, Teresa, Therese, Padre Pio, Mother Teresa, etc. Every one of these spiritual giants willingly sat at the feet of Jesus—meditating on his words, surrendering to his will and merging their awareness with his Consciousness; each in their own way.

Part of why I fell in love with Yogananda is that his teachings help me, in very practical ways, to attune myself to the Consciousness of Christ. Without Yogananda's enlightened guidance, I would not be living a Christian life; a true paradox. Thus, daily I pray for the grace to do what Yogananda teaches, to align myself to the Christ

Consciousness, and to surrender my will to God's will. I can no longer afford to do it "my way," because it visits suffering upon others, and me.

The third vow is chastity. Don't panic. Chastity does not mean celibacy. Chastity is actually living from the heart center and unleashing the power of love into our lives, not for "my" happiness or fulfillment or welfare, but for the good of the "other." The sexual drive, the power drive, and the security drive are not repressed, but function in service to the life of the heart--which is always seeking the greater good of others. Chastity takes our primal energies and transmutes them into the forces of charity, compassion and generosity. Chastity takes both the natural forces of life and God's grace, and directs them to the heart—enlivening the heart, making the heart the center of life.

Chastity is living without covetousness or greed or indifference. The fruit of chastity is always generosity. Therefore, chaste sex between a husband and wife is not primarily for the sake of a good orgasm, but the happiness of the other, the nurturing, bonding and strengthening of the relationship, for the shared experience of joy, and openness to new life.

Chastity does not create sterility. To the contrary, chastity allows the divine life to blossom in new and unexpected ways. Francis and Yogananda were chaste and celibate, yet their lives were incredibly creative, rich, robust and generative--producing fruit even to this day. The Blessed Mother was a virgin, but she said "yes" to God's extravagant request and became the "Mother of God,", as Catholic and Orthodox Christians proclaim."

Chastity even applies to our relationship with God--meaning we reach a point where we love God for the sake of loving God. We naturally desire to be generous towards God.

117

Instead of asking God to serve us, we seek to serve God. In loving God in this manner, we become God-like.

Many of us, including myself, have a difficult time opening our hearts to deeper levels of love—because we have been hurt, and naturally want to protect ourselves from more pain. If hell is anything, it is an isolated and walled-off heart. At some point in the spiritual journey, God will begin to open our hearts. The heart typically cracks open in the context of great pain, and in the experience of God's love—in the form the guru's grace, friends and a spiritual community. Once the heart is opened, we naturally become generous—which is the essence of a chaste life. The following is an entry from my journal,

"When I sat to meditate this morning, I was experiencing great discomfort. It was as if a sword was piercing my heart. The pain was excruciating. The meditation techniques helped to some degree, but not much. Finally, I lifted my gaze towards heaven and asked for help. Almost immediately discernible warmth descended upon me; and something released in my heart. My interior tension disappeared altogether. What remained was a subtle bliss, and freedom from self-absorption. Shortly thereafter, my cat jumped on my lap and rubbed his nose to my nose; and Vicki Jo came over and kissed me on the forehead. These were, I believe, kisses from God. During the remainder of the day, I felt fluid and spontaneous and loving. I imagine that the sword in the heart will return. At least now, however, I know God is doing something in and through the pain—opening my heart, of course."

The life of any sincere spiritual seeker is a "vowed" life, thus a life of renunciation. But it is also a life of supreme fulfillment. Our hearts and souls were created for the experience of God's unbounded love, and nothing other than the experience of God's unbounded love will ever satisfy our interior stirrings.

Since buying our building, deepening our silence and intensifying our commitment to Yogananda's mission, I have spent more than a few nights on my knees in search of God's wisdom, strength and guidance. The challenges involved in such an endeavor cut deep into the soul and demand a willingness to surrender everything to God's providence. The vows of poverty, chastity and obedience are helping us—the Assisi Institute----to avail ourselves to what is "Above." In other words, the vows set into motion all the forces, graces and blessings of heaven on our behalf--so that our lives can be the marriage of heaven earth. The vows of poverty, obedience and chastity are not a sacrifice, but the way of spiritual evolution and fulfillment. They lead us to the experience of God union.

Both Vicki Jo and I are amazed and humbled by the willingness of people to live by the three vows. A number of the individuals at the Assisi Institute have committed themselves to the path of renunciation, taking vows of celibacy and offering their lives as a service to God and others. We have a core group of disciples dedicated to living the vows of poverty, obedience and chastity in the context of marriage, work and family life. We have a paid staff of five who work extremely hard for very little money. And we have a community of people who generously share time, talent and treasure in the service of God. God is generously fashioning us into a "spiritual family," allowing us the privilege of serving those who hunger to live a divine life—here and now.

The outward expression of our community life takes place on Thursday nights. Nearly 80 people gather for prayer, sacred chanting, silent meditation and teaching. In addition, we also offer courses, retreats, periods of prayer and reflection, evening prayers, relic displays, spiritual direction, service projects, meditation courses, interfaith services, and more.

We have purposely avoided offering a Sunday service because we are not a church, but a spiritual community. We want people to have the opportunity to stay connected to their religious traditions.

Most importantly, we endeavor to steep ourselves in the Great Silence – becoming a living, breathing vortex of God's stillness. The world has plenty of activity and motion. It has little of God's transcendental peace. Jesus said *"My peace I give you, not as the world gives it."*[71] By our prayerful silence, we attempt to embody this peace, not for ourselves, but for the world. God's peace is not the absence of conflict, but a dynamic power or momentum that organizes creation in a wise, orderly and evolutionary manner. God's peace is the sole foundation of a peaceful and just society.

There are studies supporting the theory that contemplative prayer, in and of itself, improves societal conditions.[72] Our individual and collective behavior is always a reflection of our consciousness – what we perceive, think, feel, believe a desire, consciously or unconsciously. To go a step further, modern physics has shown us we don't exist as isolated entities. Rather, we are all part of a collective consciousness, a unified field, a gravitation vortex.[73] When a group of people come together and enter deeply into the Great Silence, they bring God's light and love into the collective consciousness of the human family, positively influencing society and culture. The deeper the silence, the more powerful the impact it has on others.

---

71 John 14:27

72 If interested in more information on spirituality and science, a good place to start is *"The Tao of Physics, by Fritjof Capra.*

73 *"The Second Coming,"* Paramahansa Yogananda, page xxviii-an inspired commentary on the four gospels.

All over the world, hermits and contemplatives are steeped in the consciousness of God's presence. Their prayerful silence, whether they are Christians or Buddhists or Hindus or Sufis or Jewish mystics, is keeping our world from spinning entirely out of control. In many of the Blessed Mother's apparitions, she tells us to pray for peace--because selfless prayer seeds the consciousness of the human family with the dynamic and organizing force of God's love, which is our only hope for real peace. In other words, prayer changes the chemistry of human consciousness.

In our simple way, we at the Assisi Institute are endeavoring to serve the world by being a community of prayerful, meditative silence. We are all imperfect, most especially me. We are, each one of us, a divine treasure in an earthen vessel--to show that the transcendent power belongs to God and not to us. We seek only to fulfill Yogananda's mission, "to re-establish God in the temple of souls through revival of the original teachings of God-communion as propounded by Christ and Krishna..."[74]

For now, God has placed me in the role of spiritual director of the Assisi Institute. I am painfully aware of my limitations, and depend heavily on the talents and good will of our members—as well as God's generous grace. Many years ago a wise Yogi explained to me that silence begins at the top, and my daily meditations were not longer for me, but for the community I serve. He also added that I had a responsibility to those who trust me to live "an impeccably honorable life."

Most importantly, I am learning the value of sacrifice— meaning that true happiness is fruit of offering all of my parts and powers to God, to be used for His purposes. When I try

---

[74] "The Second Coming of Christ: The Resurrection of the Christ Within You," Self-Realization Fellowship, published in 2004, page xxviii.

to create happiness for myself, I invariably suffer. But when my life becomes a self-offering to God, God's peace and bliss and wisdom and strength pour into me—making me a better husband, father, counselor, teacher, friend, etc. This is not only true for me, but for everyone. To the extent that we lovingly yield our lives to God, we give God permission to divinize our lives—only then do we become truly, deeply human.

Francis of Assisi perfectly captures what I believe to be my personal mission, and the mission of the Assisi Institute with these words:

"We have been called to heal wounds, to unite what has fallen apart, and to bring home those who have lost their way.[75]

---

[75] This quote is attributed to St. Francis, and was passed on to me by Father Richard OFM.

8 The Fullness of Life

These things I have spoken to you, that my joy may be in you, and that your joy may be full. - Jesus

Ever-new joy is God. - Yogananda

Not too long into my practice of Kriya Yoga, I was blessed to have a conversation with one of Yogananda's living disciples. In eager anticipation of the meeting, I prepared a list of complicated, philosophical questions—confident we would plumb the depths of esoteric mysticism. In sitting down together, I was full of excited anticipation, and hardly able to contain myself. Before I could ask my questions, however, he said, "Let us begin with silence."

So, we sat in silence; not for a minute or two, but for twenty-minutes. He broke the silence with a series of questions, "Are you meditating daily?"

To which I responded, "Yes sir."

123

"Good. Are you also studying the appropriate spiritual texts?"

"Yes."

"Are you practicing moderation in food, not eating too much or too little?"

"Well sir, food is a tough one for me but I am trying."

"By the size of your belly, I can see that you struggle with food. Keep working on it."

"Yes sir."

"Are you finding balance between work and rest, and do you go to bed at a night and wake in the morning at a consistent time?"

"Yes."

"Are you fulfilling your duties in a responsible and effective manner?"

"Yes. I think so."

"Are you a positive force in people's lives"?

"I believe so."

"Are you able to direct your sexual energy in helpful and healthy and appropriate ways?"

"Not always easy, but yes."

"Do you have a sense of God's presence in your life?"

"Absolutely!"

"Do you feel the guidance of the Guru in your life?"

"I believe so."

"Are you generally peaceful and content?"

"Yes, thank God."

"Well, it sounds like you are making good progress on your spiritual path. It's been nice talking with you."

"But sir, I had these questions I wanted to ask you."

"Do you have serious problems?"

"No. My questions are more theological in nature."

"Are they essential to your spiritual growth?"

"I don't think so."

"Good. Just keep meditating and God will answer your theological questions, if He thinks they should be answered.

"Can I have your blessing?" I asked.

"No." he answered.

"Why?"

Looking me straight in the eye, he said, "Because you are capable of receiving a blessing directly from God, through your own prayers."

He got up, shook my hand and left the room. I didn't know whether to be pleased or irritated. In time, however, I understood the wisdom of his council. The spiritual path is less about theological theory and more about faithfulness, vigilance and the development of virtue—the fruit of which is an ever deepening sense of communion with God, increased wisdom and an expanding capacity to love others.

The path of Kriya Yoga --and any legitimate contemplative spirituality -- unfolds according to certain disciplines or practices. The **first discipline** centers on the need to cultivate a conscious **attunement** with one's guru.[76] A great saint has the ability, even after leaving the body, to remain present to his or her devotees. Their presence is literally a vortex of God's grace—having the ability to elevate the devotee's consciousness beyond karma, habit and conditioning.[77] In short, the guru helps their devotees to

---

[76] A guru of the highest order is literally an embodiment of God's grace—whether they are in the body or not. Attunement to the energy and consciousness of a God-realized guru transforms our energy and consciousness. In essence, we become what we focus on. As the "Word made flesh," Jesus is the preeminent guru or savior for Christians. This is not to say, however, that other spiritual traditions do have saints or spiritual masters capable of elevating the consciousness of their devotees. Ultimately, it is the same "Christ-Consciousness" or "Christ-Logos" operating in and through the legitimate saints of the various religious traditions. On what authority do I say this? Jesus said, *"You will know them by their fruit."* If a spiritual teacher demonstrates overwhelming virtue, faith, wisdom, joy, compassion, love, and their teachings brings others to a level of God communion, what other proof is needed?

[77] There is much misunderstanding about karma. Karma is not "pay back," but the tendency to experience life according to certain habitual tendencies. Only God's grace, along with our willingness, can trump the force of karma.

experience deeper and deeper levels of God-communion.

Attunement to a God-realized guru can take various forms: prayerful study of their teachings, prayers for help and guidance, serving the guru's mission, sacramental rituals, meditating on the guru's image, and obedience to the guru's injunctions. In our culture, however, obedience has become a dirty word. Yet, Jesus said, *"If you love me, obey my commandments."* [78] Obedience to a God-realized guru is actually the willingness to avail ourselves to truth—truth alone has the power to set us free. The willingness to surrender to the guru's wise, loving counsel is essential for spiritual growth. The bottom line is that we all need a "power greater than ourselves" to save us from ourselves; this is not a point of shame, but freedom.

The bond between Guru and disciple is an eternal one — meaning that once it is established, it cannot be broken. Jesus said, *"...and this is the will of Him who sent me, that I shall not lose nothing of all that He has given me, but raise it up on the last day."* [79] Though we might miss the mark many, many times a day, the guru neither loses sight of us nor abandons us—meaning that the guru's grace is always available to us, waiting only for our prayerful surrender. Even if we descend into the deepest hell, we are never beyond the reach of the guru's God-saturated grace. [80]

---

[78] John 14:15

[79]: John 6:39

[80] Gregory of Nyssa and Maximus the Confessor, recognized saints in both Catholic and Orthodox Churches, maintained a belief that in the end all people would be gathered into God. Neither of these saints was condemned for their positions on universal salvation.

Personally speaking, the only way I am capable of fulfilling my God-given responsibilities with any degree of wisdom and love is by relying on Jesus' grace, Yogananda's wisdom and Francis' inspiration. Often, I find myself on my knees— praying for guidance, so that I can be a channel of God's grace. I deeply suspect that by the time I leave my body, my knees will be covered with thick calluses.

The **second Kriya Discipline** is **meditation.** The deepest, most essential value in a meditation practice is not improved health or mental concentration, but the ever-deepening awareness of God's presence. Without a regular meditation practice, our sense of God's presence will be inconsistent, at best. Meditation opens our awareness to God's peace, God's wisdom and God's love. Meditation is, quite literally, the practice of dipping ourselves in Divinity.

Once conscious contact with God has been established, we can learn to maintain this contact while working, when interacting with others and in all aspects of our lives. This means that God's presence becomes a perpetual font of inspiration and wisdom—guiding us in all of our affairs, including our most mundane concerns. Through a discipline of daily meditation, God's presence can become a stabilized aspect of our own consciousness.

There is a danger, however, that can emerge relative to a daily meditation practice. Namely, we can think that we have arrived—believing that we have reached the zenith of God realization. We must remain humble and always open to deeper levels of God-realization. No matter how long we have been meditating, we must always approach our spiritual practices with a beginner's mind. Yogananda said,

> **"Stillness has many screens...You must never think that you have found the last stillness, the last realization or joy. Whenever you feel you have reached the last climax of stillness, realization or joy, seek further, and you will enter into a finer, deeper state.... God is inexhaustible."[81]**

The **third Kriya discipline** is **prayer**. I must confess, however, that during the first few years of my Kriya Yoga meditation practice I virtually stopped praying altogether. I was so intent on meditating, that I ignored the need for prayer. Eventually, I came to realize that meditation is the left lung of the spiritual life and prayer the right lung—both being essential to the spiritual life.

True prayer is not about asking for things, but for God— God's will, God's guidance, God's wisdom, God's strength, God's peace, God's love, God's grace, God's presence. The bottom line is that the spiritual life is about the loving union of two free, independent wills—God's will and our will. God's love is always being extended to us; prayer is our way of saying "yes" to God's love and extending ourselves to God—which has the effect of changing the chemistry of our consciousness, of our emotions, of our hearts and those situations in which we find ourselves.

Being the spiritual director of the Assisi Institute is, at times, a daunting task. On one occasion, when facing some unfair

---

[81] "Rajarsi Janakananda, A Great Western Yogi" page 120, Self-Realization Fellowship, 1996.

and unsavory criticism from an outside party, I sat prayerfully in front of a large image of Yogananda -- for over an hour. Again and again I tearfully prayed, "*Please guide me. If I am doing something wrong show me. Let me know that it is you guiding the Assisi Institute.*" Immediately after praying, a man showed up at the Assisi Institute and gave me a check for $1,952. After thanking him for his generous gift, I asked why the check was written for such an unusual amount.

He replied, "Because that was the year of Yogananda's death. It just seemed right to give you a donation for that amount."

I was happy to receive the money on behalf of the Assisi Institute, but I was more pleased receive Yogananda's blessing.

Yogananda tells us to pray from the "...*bottom of our souls.*"[82] To pray from the bottom of our souls is to pray with utter sincerity -- for God is radical sincerity. Thus, to experience prayerful contact with God we must be sincere! When our sincerity is united with God's sincerity, our words and actions become powerful — because the very life-blood of God begins to flow through our spiritual veins. We become our prayers; and we also become God's living prayer. In the face of such prayerful and unified sincerity, God's angels bow.

The **fourth Kriya** discipline is **right living.** Right living is not earning God's love or an attempt to perfect the personality. The spiritual life always begins with God's free, unmerited grace. In other words, God always makes the first move—a move of unconditional love, inviting us into Divine

---

[82] "How you can talk with God," Paramahansa Yogananda. Page 34: Self-Realization Fellowship, published in 1957.

fellowship. God's love, however, should not be understood as impotent pleasantness. It is, quite literally, the Breath of God moving into the deepest crevices our lives as a purposeful, organizing power. This means that the energy of God's presence begins to reshape the fundamental patterns of our lives. We begin to live our lives differently, not to make ourselves worthy of God's love; but as a response to God's love--to keep us open, receptive and available to deeper and deeper levels of God's love.

Early on my practice of Kriya Yoga, I hit a stretch of extreme busyness. For a number of weeks I stopped meditating, eating properly, getting enough rest, etc. I justified my lack of balance—otherwise known as right living—because my busyness was serving a noble cause. At the end of a few weeks, I was exhausted, irritable and far removed from the peace of God's presence. So, I arranged a meeting with a spiritual mentor, to ask for his guidance.

As soon as we sat down, he could see that there was a problem. He then asked, "What's going on?"

"I think I am experiencing a 'dark night' of the soul.

"What does that mean?" he asked.

"It means that God is withholding His consolations from me. I am no longer experiencing His presence. He must be doing this to purify me, so that I can go deeper in my spiritual life."

Chuckling, my mentor replied, "This is no dark night of the soul experience. What's going on is that you are exhausted, overworked and overwhelmed. Your nervous system is frazzled. You cannot consistently experience God's presence if your nervous system is on overload. Take today and tomorrow off. Sleep as much as you want, do some gentle meditating, eat a healthy meal or two, and watch a ballgame on the television."

What he said made complete sense. I did what he told me to do, and felt much better. The bottom line is that God's intelligence permeates every grain of creation. This means that life, even one's spiritual life, unfolds according to an established blueprint or template or pattern—often referred to as the "natural order." Spiritual growth unfolds, in part, to the degree that our lives are in alignment with the natural order — because such alignment allows the seed of God, buried within us, to blossom to a ripe fullness. Thus, "right living" is alignment to God's template for creation: keeping the Ten Commandments, not eating too little or too much, finding a balance between work and rest, maintaining a consistent schedule, grounding our lives in wholesome activities, remembering to play and laugh, the right use of our sexual energy, spiritual study, family time, etc. Right living is the fruit of God's grace, and the order necessary to allow our lives to be metabolized more deeply into the Divine Life.

The next **Kriya discipline is service.** The spiritual life is, in part, the willingness to transcend self-absorption, to live for something greater than narrow self-interest, to live for God's causes. Selfless service makes us larger, in that we are serving something larger — yes, God. In short, we become what we serve. Through selfless service, our lives become divine. Service opens us to the momentum of God's Spirit; the more we serve, the more the wind is at our back — meaning that the very energies of God inspire and support our noble endeavors. An example of the power of service can be found in one of the tenets of Alcoholics Anonymous; often formulated as "one drunk helping another drunk to stay sober." In serving another person's sobriety, paradoxically, the alcoholic deepens his or her own sobriety—because what comes through us to help others, also blesses us. In the words of Jesus,

"Give, and it will be given to you; good measure, pressed down, shaken together, running over, will be put into your lap. For the measure you give will be the measure you get back."[83]

Through much of my adult life, I wanted to help others. I became a psychotherapist, for example, to serve others. Until my immersion in Kriya Yoga, however, something vital was missing. Specifically, my service was compartmentalized. Yes, I tried my best to serve my clients, my sons, and my friends. Yet, I was keeping an essential portion of my life, indeed my soul, for myself—grasping for a personal, private happiness that was always beyond my reach. I certainly wanted to give to others, to love God--but not too much. I was trying, vainly, to live a so-called normal life.

A profoundly clarifying moment for me came amidst a very pleasant, joyous experience within the Assisi Institute. Namely, we had just completed our annual three-hour Christmas meditation service; and people were partaking happily in wonderful food, spiritual conversation and one another's presence. Their joy was palpable. As I watched in amazement, a series of poignant thoughts bubbled up into my

---

83 Luke 6: 38

awareness:

"Look at what's going on here, Craig. These people trust you and are endeavoring to give their lives entirely to God. They believe what you tell them about God, Christ and Yogananda. This is your life -- what you are meant to do. This is what God wants you to do, until your last breath. There are no other jobs to apply for, no transfers to seek, no alternative dreams to follow — no turning back. Everything in your life has been a preparation for this work, and it is going to take everything you have, a total commitment. You can't hold anything back. Every bit of your energy must be given to God, for His purposes. You must rely on God, totally."

How did I respond to this stream of interior thought? I took a deep breath, and said, *"Yes."* Strangely, I did not feel fear or dread, but relief. I simply accepted, as best as I could, my marching orders. Did I know then what it all meant? No. Do I know what it all means today? Not really. Do I feel up to the task? Not entirely. I just know that God is faithful and that my job is to willingly give everything I have to the service to which God has called me.

Obviously, not everyone is called to lead a spiritual organization or be a missionary or a monk or a nun. However, everyone is called to spend their lives in service of something greater than themselves, to embrace willingly their God-given duties, and to do ordinary tasks with extraordinary love — doing it all in God, because of God, for God. This is how our lives become divinized, period.

The **final Kriya discipline** is **surrender.** Complete surrender is not possible at first -- which is to say that surrender is a process. What is surrendered? Everything! Our bodies are surrendered to God, our sexual energy is surrendered to God, our emotions are surrendered to God, our thoughts are surrendered to God, our desires are surrendered to God, our imagination is surrendered to God, and our will is surrendered to God. This is not so that God will annihilate us, but so that God can divinize all aspects of our existence. When our lives are surrendered to God, deeply, we allow God to break into our lives in miraculous ways, releasing divine forces and trumping our karmic tendencies.

Surrender, however, is not a passive affair. This means that we must continually maintain the "willingness" to surrender everything to God — our failures and triumphs, our joy and suffering, our virtues and sins. Everything belongs to God because we belong to God, wholly and entirely. Our willingness to surrender is the necessary precondition for the influx of divine energy into our lives. In the final analysis, the spiritual life is the surrender of our entire being to the mysterious will of God — just as a lover willingly yields herself to her beloved. Surrendering to God's will, even when it appears to make no sense at all, does not lead to a sparse or joyless existence. Rather, surrendering to God is the exclusive path to our highest, noblest and happiest possibilities.

It is important to note that even the best spiritual practices can only lead us to the gate of the temple, never into the temple. At the gate of the temple we are capable of experiencing many consolations: peace and stillness and joy and sweetness and even a sense of communion with God. There remains, however, a sense of distance between God and us—ever so slight. Inside the metaphorical temple, however, there is union with God.

Union with God is the experience of the Divine beyond concepts or images or feelings. The "I" of the personality disappears altogether; what remains is the simple marriage of the soul to God: a union of unspeakable, pure love—whereby the two become one. Where we end and God begins becomes blurred, even nonexistent. There is just the experience of pure divinity. In the words of Teresa of Avila,

"The spiritual marriage, on the other hand, it is like rain falling from the sky into a river or pool.

There is nothing but water. It is impossible to divide the sky-water from the land water. When a little stream enters the sea, who could separate the waters back again? Think of a bright light pouring into a room from two large windows: it enters from different places but becomes one light."[84]

No matter how hard we try, we cannot force the experience of union to occur. It comes as a gift or grace from God, and unfolds when God so chooses. We can nurture the willingness for union, but we can't make it happen. Through the process of purification, however, God strips us of attachments, desires, aversions, concepts and positions; this eventually brings us to the awareness of our soul's purest suppleness—which is the precondition for the experience of union. Then, at the auspicious moment, God lovingly suspend our capacity to think, to imagine and to desire; and what remains is simple, loving and undiluted union. It is

---

[84] "The Interior Castle" by St. Teresa of Avila, translated by Mirabai Starr, page 270

somewhat akin to being in a deep, dreamless state of sleep, but being fully conscious.

Among the fruits of a stabilized sense of God union are: humility, a deep desire to please God and to serve God, an enhanced ability to love others--even when they are cruel and hurtful towards us, the willingness to speak the truth, deep peace and inner silence, the ability to gracefully endure trials, joy and freedom from the fear of death. We were created to live our lives within the context of God-union; thus, union with God is our inevitable destiny in this life or the next. Everything that happens to us is a preparation for union, with God.

In closing, my life is busier than ever. Yet, it is also becoming increasingly simple, happy and full. The first thing my wife and I do in the morning is meditate, often for two hour at a sitting—concluding with an inspired reading and prayers of gratitude to God and the gurus. We have a cup of coffee, chow down some breakfast and dash off to a full day of seeing clients, facilitating meetings, and teaching classes. At the end of the day, we come home, make an attempt to exercise, fix dinner, watch an occasional television program, read, pray and sleep. Our discretionary time is largely spent with family, and tending to our home and garden. We laugh a lot, work a lot, and love a lot. God has blessed us with a full and rich life.

There remains within me, however, a "percolating wound." I used to pray to have this wound removed. Now, however, I see this wound as a point of vulnerability—yes, an opening whereby God floods my heart and soul with heavenly light and wisdom. It is the very portal by which God enters my life. As such, my wound has become a great blessing—availing me to the experience of God's love. Ah, the mystery of God's providence.

Despite my many imperfections, I pray that my story serves as a window into God's extravagant love. I pray you know that you are God's "image" and "likeness," not theoretically, but as an actual experience. I pray you live your life from God's "Great Silence," the sole source of everything good, worthwhile, and noble. I pray you allow God's light to descend into your deepest depths, so that you might be purified, divinized and liberated. I pray you know you have been created for delight and an extraordinary life. I pray you know the absolute joy of serving God's purposes. I pray you experience your life not as a cosmic roll of the dice, but as God's living inspiration. I pray you know you have been loved into existence — by a God who is Love. And I pray you know and experience what Jesus knew and experienced, and offered to all of his followers: "*I and the Father are one.*" God bless you all!

I leave you with my favorite prayer from Francis of Assisi:

> "Most high and glorious God,
> Bring light to the darkness of my heart.
> Give me right faith, certain hope and perfect charity,
> Insight and wisdom-- so I can always observe your holy
> and true command. Amen"

The Assisi Institute

The Assisi Institute is a meditation and retreat center and a spiritual community. We host services, classes, retreats and other events to enhance spiritual understanding, promote peace and experience greater levels of communion with God.

The Assisi Institute Mission Statement

The Assisi Institute is dedicated to supporting individuals who seek a deeper relationship with God. Through the harmonious integration of Kriya Yoga and mystical Christianity, we nurture a sacred community of meditation, contemplative inquiry and compassionate living.

Living Grace Daily Reflections

Receive inspiration in your email inbox! Composed by Craig Bullock, these daily reflections provide spiritual insight for embodying grace in the modern world. To register for *Living Grace* and The Assisi Institute mailing list, please visit: www.assisi-institute.org

The Assisi Institute

1400 North Winton Rd.
Rochester, NY 14609
(585) 473-8731 phone
info@assisi-institute.org
www.assisi-institute.org

Appendix: Commonly Asked Questions

Is Kriya Yoga a religion?

No! The word "yoga" means union. The word "kriya" means action. Thus, Kriya Yoga focuses on certain actions that help to facilitate the experience of union with God. The routines and disciplines and practices of Kriya Yoga can be integrated into any traditional religious path. Kriya Yoga is not primarily driven by beliefs. Those beliefs associated with Kriya Yoga are universal to all theistic religions; for example, belief in God, the existence of the soul, union with God as the goal of life, compassionate living, etc.

How does the Kriya Yoga technique work?

We come to God not as angels, but as human beings—as embodied human beings. As the bible states, our bodies are "temples of the Holy Spirit." In other words, grace always builds on nature. To be stabilized in a state of "God union" or "God realization," it is most helpful to have the nervous system functioning in an optimal manner. The Kriya Yoga lifestyle helps us to create balance and order and peace; and is therefore the foundation for the direct experience of God. The Kriya Yoga meditation technique helps to purify the nervous system--so as to allow it to handle and hold more and more divine energy.

Where can I learn about the kriya technique?

Ideally, it is best to learn the meditation technique from someone authorized to teach it. Typically, one must go through a period of preparation prior to "Kriya Initiation," to maximize the benefits of the technique.

What is Kriya Initiation?

During the Kriya initiation two things takes place: The Kriya technique is taught, and a blessing is given—accompanied by the "laying on of hands."

What is the blessing about?

In the blessing, there is an attunement that takes place between the person being initiated and the lineage of the gurus. In other words, God's grace is given; this grace elevates the person being initiated into a higher, more elevated state of consciousness. Though personal effort is an essential element of the path, God's grace is what makes spiritual realization or transformation possible. The best technique in the world will bring us to the gate of the temple, but only God's grace brings us into the temple—into the experience of "God Union."

Can Jesus be my guru?

Yes! Again, there is nothing in the Kriya Yoga lifestyle or technique that contradicts Jesus' teachings. Christ is very present to all people, regardless of their religious affiliation. The more we present ourselves to Jesus, the more present is his grace. It is that simple. Jesus can belong to us, if we are willing to belong to him.

Aren't you committing idolatry by having a devotion to Yogananda?

Not at all! Is a Catholic committing idolatry by having a devotion to the Blessed Mother or St. Francis? The answer, obviously, is "No." We are devoted to a particular saint for the simple reason that he or she attunes us to the Holy Spirit. Most saints spend their time in heaven doing good on earth—functioning as vortexes of grace, God's grace to be exact. I think it is silly to believe that only the Catholic Church can produces saints. I have met a few Hindu holy men and women, for example, who consistently exhibit saint-like qualities--such as love, compassion, wisdom, peace, virtue, courage, strength, etc. When I view a video of the Dali Lama or read his words, I am immediately uplifted. Only a saint has the power to consistently impact other people in a positive and uplifting manner. I base my devotion to Yogananda on my own, personal experience. Since being initiated into Kriya Yoga and following his practical recommendations, my life has been transformed. Yogananda has made me a better Christian. I don't think that Jesus is jealous of my devotion to Yogananda, at all. In fact, I believe that Jesus led me to Yogananda. Great saints do not belong to a particular religion; they belong to everyone!

What is your definition of a saint?

That would be a long discussion. For simplicity sake, suffice it to say that a saint is not someone who is lost in ecstasy or has perfected their personality. Rather, a saint is an individual who never forgets God; and seeks to be an instrument of God's truth, beauty and goodness in all situations.

Do you still consider yourself to be Catholic?

Yes! For me, there is no contradiction between my practice of Kriya Yoga and my Catholicism. Both the "Eucharist" and "Confession" continue to be sources of profound grace. For example, Kriya Yoga has deepened my appreciation of

Christ's presence in the "Breaking of the Bread." Every time I receive "Holy Communion" I experience my personal consciousness as being metabolized into the very consciousness of Christ.

Isn't Christ the only path to God?

Yes, but one must have a proper understanding of "Christ." Christ was not Jesus' last name, but a title or designation given to him; because he perfectly embodied the Christ Consciousness—Christ Consciousness is the "mind" or "logos" or "Intelligence" of God working within creation, to bring about the spiritual evolution of the human race. St. Teresa of Avila, while in a state of mystical union, spoke of experiencing the "formless Christ." Because of this, she was accused of being a heretic--until a respected theologian came to her rescue by noting that a great saint had written about the formless Christ. If we read the Torah or the Bhagavad Gita or the Dao De Jing with an open mind, we will readily recognize the formless Christ at work in these scriptural texts. Am I saying that all paths reflect the same level of light? No. What I am saying is that Christ Consciousness permeates every nook and cranny of creation, and is present in all legitimate spiritual paths—working to bring us all home. Indeed, God's love is extravagantly large.

Do you consider yourself to be a guru?

Hardly! I am an imperfect servant of Christ and Francis and Yogananda—trying to faithfully represent their teachings, so as to assist people on their journey to "God Realization."

Can you sum the most important elements in the spiritual life?

God is simple. The spiritual path is simple: surrender everything to God, pray and meditate, stay close to the silence, and seek to be an instrument of God's love in all situations.

I choose you ♡

27183970R00093